Brave

Stephanie Thompson

DEDICATION

To my beautiful children. So that you will understand better your mother's life story. To my grown daughter, may you always know how awesome and strong you are. That you are more than capable of accomplishing your goals. To my younger son, that you will read this as an adult and understand my work to support healthy families when you were growing up. You are also awesome, strong, and more than capable of whatever you put your mind to do. May you both continue to grow in love, faith, and courage. I love you.

CONTENTS

ACKNOWLEDGMENTS

To my friends, who championed me during the process of writing this book. Going back into my past to tell my story was at times heartbreaking. Your support gave me courage to continue.

1 MAD ALL THE TIME

When I was growing up, I had big dreams for my life. I dreamed of living in New York, in a luxury apartment in a tall building with lots of windows. I saw myself as a business executive with a large office, happily doing my work behind a beautiful desk. I never saw myself on food stamps or applying for Medicaid to pay for the delivery of my first child with no help from her father. I never saw myself starting over from scratch. I never imagined that I would be in that position. I cried at the doctor's office while sitting on the exam table, waiting to be seen for my first prenatal visit. I was running out of money and emotionally drained. What I did have was a love for the child I was carrying.

I wanted to bring my child into the world and provide a loving and prosperous life for her. I wanted to protect her and teach her all the lessons I missed and then some. How did I get here?

"You're a fool if you think anybody wants you!" My mother told me since my earliest memory.

"You are so dumb! She would say.

"Ignorance is bliss". She said.

"Witchy poo" was what she called me, comparing me to the girlfriend of the unavailable man she was dating at the time. She hated her. She hated me.

"Bald head witchy poo!" She would scream when she was really mad about something. I never knew what she was so mad about. She yelled with such anger that I trembled inside. She was disgusted with me.

"You all ruined my life! She yelled to me and my younger siblings. I was 12 years old. I was the oldest of four children, all with different fathers, being raised by our single mother. We adored her. But she didn't feel the same way about us.

"I would be living in a glass house if it wasn't for all of you!" She yelled. We were too scared to move. We were left open to her insults with no protection. Her words stung like a belt.

Her words hurt our feelings. Why did she hate us? I still don't have the answer. And somedays it still hurts. I believed what she said, she was my mother, she would not lie to us. I seemed to move around the house like I had a heavy weight on my shoulders, unsure, my mind spinning, afraid of each step I made fearing I would make her mad.

She was mad most of the time regardless of what I did. She was growling it seemed to me. She almost always frowned. Sometimes she looked like the anger was taking over her. It seemed like it was just beneath the surface at all times except when she was looking in the Sears & Roebuck catalog. At those times she would lay on the couch on her stomach with her legs up and crossed above her back, swinging them back and forth in a relaxed way, the catalog on the floor. She turned each page slowly. She was calm. She looked happy.

Out the door I went. The pasture, the creek running through it, the plum trees, and the blackberry bushes were my saving grace. I loved the fresh air, the wide open yard, and the trees to climb. I loved the sound of the wind blowing through the green leaves of early summer, it was a peaceful sound. Even though we did not see anyone but our mother and our siblings for weeks, it didn't bother me, at first. As long as I had our land and I was able to get away from the chaos inside, I thought I was okay.

My mother's rules were hard. There were certain ways to do everything and punishment if we didn't get it just right. There was no way to win.

"Pull the sheet tighter!"

"Fold the towels like this!" She said and took the towels from us in a quick angry way.

"Fold the towels the way they should be folded!" She yelled while giving a demonstration. Yelling and cursing and growling. I was so scared of her. She'd make us fold the towels again, until she was satisfied. If we did it incorrectly, she'd hit us with whatever she had in her hand or could pick up first. A broom, an extension cord, a shoe.

She hit hard like she was trying to make sure we never forgot it. She just couldn't stand imperfection. Trying was not good enough. There was no grace for learning, we had to do it right the first time or else.

If we were making her bed, she would yank us back away from the corner of the bed and insult us terribly.

"Do it again!" She'd yell. We could never get it perfect. Then she would push us away and take the sheet like a wild woman. She'd yank, pull and tuck the flat sheet under the foot of the heavy mattress, crease the corners and tuck it under the side of the mattress.

"That is a hospital corner!" She yelled in anger. It was a

scary time for me and my brother. He was two years younger than me. Afraid of her next move, we stood against the wall, frozen.

"You'll never be anything!" She told us. The insults flew. It was her bedroom and it still had to be cleaned, to perfection. Making her bed was just the beginning.

She had pushed trash under her bed, mixed with catalogs, magazines, chicken bones, dirty plates, and cups. She placed an empty laundry basket in the middle of the room to put the things in that she swept from under her bed and around her room.

"Just throw everything in there!" she pointed and yelled, motioning toward the basket. "Sort it out later!" She used the straw broom to push the things from under the bed into a large pile. There were so many things. Then she'd sweep the floor.

We weren't allowed to use a dust pan.

"Use your hands!" She screamed as we sat on our knees getting up the last of the dirt from her floor. She'd tear a piece of cardboard from an empty cereal box.

"Hold it like this!" She screamed, pressing the cardboard into my hand as I kneeled near the dirt she'd swept into a pile. It wasn't a lot of dirt, but it was often wet because she swept everything into that pile, spilt bath water, and whatever was on her floor. She did the same thing when she swept in the kitchen. She particularly grossed me out when she swept the kitchen table with that broom.

Trying to place the cardboard at the right angle, I feared the broom coming down on my back. I tried to focus on it and on her. Looking up at her was an automatic hit with the broom. She swept the dirt across the cardboard up over my hand, I hated how that felt. She did that every time. She could tell it bothered me, but I didn't say so. If something bothered us, she did it more and exaggerated doing it with no consideration of how it made us feel. It was like she enjoyed making us feel bad.

"You dumb ass fool! She yelled if some of the dirt did not get on the makeshift dust pan.
"Didn't I tell you to do it like this? She'd grab it, pressing it to the floor at an angle. I tried again.

She threatened us if she didn't get the dirt on the cardboard, "I'll knock you in the head if you don't hold it right!" Down to the last bit of dirt she'd say,

"Use your hands!"

"Cup your hands like this!" She cupped the palms of her hands as if she was scooping up something. My brother and I cupped our hands, we took turns, trying to scoop up every grain of dirt up.

After the dirt was up, we had to sort the items in the basket, by now it was full of shoes, papers, dishes, and clothes that were clean and dirty. Everything had to be put up, in its place. The dirty clothes put in a pile to be washed.

Most of the time she ate in her bedroom where she would take her dinner walking past us without stopping and telling us, "You all better go get something" as she burst through the kitchen door, plate and huge plastic cup of coffee in her hand.

She burst through the door, yelling as she walked past us sitting on the floor in the living room then through the other door, taking a quick turn through her bedroom door and closing it with force behind her. That was our clue that we could eat what she had cooked, still on the stove in the pot or skillet.

She would not come out of her room for several hours, sometimes we did not see her until the next day. She shouted commands and banged on her thin, hollow bedroom wall, it rumbled like thunder, to tell us to, "Turn that TV down!" or "Go to bed!", sounding mad and out of control.

At times she would shout commands from her bedroom in a less intense tone, she sounded nervous, her voice shaking, like it took all her energy to tell us what to do. She sounded overwhelmed. She sounded like she was all alone and even scared at times.

Most days it was full-blown fussing and cursing. She cursed us out like we were grown-ups who understood what those words meant. She cursed strongly, with force. A few times I'm sure we were getting on her nerves fussing among ourselves and deserved a good cursing.

I tried to keep the peace as much as I could. She would fly into a screaming violent whooping spell when she had had enough. I can remember two whoopings that I and my brother two years younger than me, got for fighting. I wanted to beat him up for taking things from me. He was so aggressive and liked to fight. I was intent on showing him he could not walk over me. We both got a whooping. I always thought that was unfair because I had been standing up for myself.

I learned quickly that my needs were not important. Just doing what my mother told me to do and not making any waves, that was it. Another time I tangled with him over something. He had a lot of anger and he knew a lot of fighting moves. But I could fight just as well as he could, and we both got a whooping. It may have been from the wrestling we watched on Saturdays.

My mother would tell me, "You have to ignore a fool", as if she knew what my brother had done, but it was my responsibility to do better than him. She'd fuss at me for his behavior, blaming me somehow. She'd call me names and him too. I stopped fighting. I started ignoring him.

I started to see how I could please my mother. How I could be good. How to act in a way that she approved of.

When I stopped fighting with my brother, I think I lost some of my spirit, my fight spirit. My mother taught me that fighting was wrong, that I should walk away. Her whoopings for me fighting were worse than the fights themselves. I gave up. Over time, I became easily intimidated.

I began to be that way at school too. Anybody could say anything to me or about me in front of others and I would not say a word. I used to talk back and get into arguments with the bullies in my class but, I was starting to pull back.

If I did say something, I quickly became fearful that if I got in trouble at school, I would get it worse at home.

I was hurting on the inside and felt I had no right to say a word no matter how it hurt. I was bullied all the time at school, on the school bus, and anytime I was around other children. They never hit me, but called me names. My short hair was a main topic for them, "bald head, nappy head," were the top names. When my skin started breaking out, they called me "bumpy face".

We eventually did understand my mother's curse words. They were the same words I saw scratched on the bathroom stalls in the gym at Walker school. The girl's bathroom was where the older girls went to smoke and the bathroom door and wall were full of curse words. It was where they talked tough about all sorts of things.

My mother's words to us were like those. They were ruthless. She didn't mince words. What came up came out.

In a matter of minutes she'd go from wild madness to sadness that was so heavy she would lie in her bed and sleep all day, get up for a few minutes, then go back to bed until the next day. She might not say a word to us.

Sometimes she was in her bedroom for days or at least we did not see her when she came out. She wouldn't come out until we were sleep or gone to school, I could tell by the things she moved around when I got up the next day or got home from school. Or the dirty plates and cups she left behind on the coffee table in the living room.

There were always chicken bones or other food between the couch cushions. It was not from the kids because we ate in the kitchen.

Other times late in the night when I couldn't sleep, I would hear her crying or talking to herself about work or people she was mad at. She was always mad at somebody or hurt by what another grown-up had said to her. Her feelings were hurt easily. She could dish it out but she couldn't take it when someone said the smallest thing to her. She wanted to be perfect.

We didn't mind when she went to her room because we were left alone. No screaming, no cursing, no being called mean names. We could take a breath for a minute, knowing she would be back but, for then we ate, we played, we did homework, we watched TV. Until she hit the uninsulated paneled wall that was between her bedroom and the living room and the yelling began again.

My job was to keep the children, to watch them while she slept, or if she was off work and up, while watched her soap operas. I had to be right there in case she called me to do something. I was either in the same room with her or within shouting distance knowing that I had to stop immediately what I was doing and run to do whatever she said. Even if it was just to bring her a glass of cold water as she sat on the couch talking to her sisters when they came to visit.

My ears were always alert for her orders. But, nothing was ever good enough. Maybe the glass of water was in the wrong glass or I spilt some as I walked fast to get it to her knowing if I took too long I would get that mean look. It was such a mean hateful look. I always knew that whatever mistake I made while her sisters were visiting, she would get me when they left.

She would wait until I wasn't expecting it and she would say all the things I had done wrong or what she felt I should have done better.

I was nervous before the company came, cleaning every inch of the house, chopping vegetables, washing dishes, assisting her every move in the kitchen. I was worn out but still excited when their cars packed with cousins finally showed up.

But I tipped around the whole time with my ears open for my mother. I did not know what fun was at a family gathering. I began to hate gatherings. They were too much work. They were too painful for me.

Her high standards…

I was in charge of my little sister's hair. I liked combing her hair. My mother hated the way I did it. She would say it looked "country" or some other crazy thing, letting me know it was not the way it should be. No matter how hard I tried or how much time I worked to get my sister's hair to look nice, my mother complained.

"You're so ignorant!" "Folks look at you like you a fool!" She said looking at my sister's hair.

Her hair was soft and thick and a little wavy. Her skin was a pretty chocolate and she had a beautiful, warm smile. She was a pretty little girl.

Since she was not a toddler anymore, maybe in the first grade by then, my mother had taken little interest in her. She was beginning to ridicule her too. When she was little, my mother dressed her in cute clothes and was tickled by her dancing when the music for Sanford and Sons came on the TV. She was a happy child then. Something had changed with my mother. As the years went on, she became more bitter, accusing us and others of far out things. She stopped taking interest in her appearance, walking around most days in her oldest house dress or her black half-slip pulled up to her shoulders like a halter dress, her hair not combed.

She stopped cleaning the house, except on those days when she made us clean every inch as she raged and complained.

Then there was the sadness. It would come on suddenly. She looked like she had the problems of the world on her shoulders. Her eyes glazed over, her shoulders drooping, her voice trembling. She would retreat to her bedroom.

Our house not our home…

The house we stayed in was not my home, it never felt like we should be there. According to my mother, we should be grateful to have the basics including toothpaste and deodorant. She made us work for them. How much we used was monitored.

She kept us in a state of fear that we would be thrown out by our granddaddy at any time and that we didn't deserve any better. "Crazy ass children!" "Always in the way!" She said often. She called us, "Pitiful fools" and that we "Did not have enough sense to know it".

"Po fool," was one of her favorite things to say to me or my siblings when she was singling one of us out, the one she was ridiculing at the time. "Po fool", she'd say. She talked about me the most.

When I didn't do a thing exactly, I mean exactly the way she said it, which was almost all the time, she would get violent. Her commands were precise, but her directions were above us, and hard to follow. We didn't know what she wanted or we'd be so busy trying to do all that she commanded that we couldn't do it all. That enraged her.

In the truck, she used that time to fuss at us like a captive audience. She fussed about everything. She drove like she was scared all the time, complaining that we were crowding her. I squeezed closer to my siblings to give her more room.

She acted like she was going to drive off the road, which scared us. I rode looking at the road and the ditch, and the curves, hoping she would stay on the road. I was tired by the time we got to where we were going and there was still work to be done.

One day she hit me in my chest so hard I was overwhelmed, I grabbed my chest, trying to catch my breath. Stunned, I could not move. It was because in my panic to get all the clothes on the back of the truck to take to the laundromat in town, I forgot to put the box of washing powder on there. She was shouting and cursing. Telling me how stupid I was. "Stupid fool!" "I'll beat your ass, now I got to drive all the way back to get that damn washing powder!" She shouted. I was scared from then on to ride in the truck with her. We were packed in the cab of a 1974 Ford pickup truck.

2 TWO PEOPLE

Then the phone would ring and her tone would change into a super kind, pleasant voice, speaking clearly, with laughs in between if it was a person she knew. If it was a stranger or bill collector, she would still be polite, even toned, but no laughs. She spoke like we still lived in the city, in Chicago, she talked "proper".

But while she was talking she would be frowning and piercing her lips saying things to us without words, "Sit your ass down, shut-up!" waving her arm aggressively as if to say if I was not on this phone I would hurt you.

We were not allowed to have fun. Not allowed to laugh. She couldn't stand it. She called any laughter except to say "ha ha", then quit, silly and country. "Ha ha", she'd demonstrate, sounding like a rich person who was not amused. That was the only acceptable way people should laugh. "Not all that loud HEE HEE HA HA..." She said mimicking someone laughing loudly.

I still loved her and wanted so badly for her to approve of me, of us. But, it was getting harder for me not to question, in my mind, why she said the things she said and acted the way she did. I knew something was wrong, very wrong, but I did not know what. I just knew that when I was around her, I felt shame, nervous, and afraid.

We had to act like we were perfect, so others, or "they" would think we were the model children. That she didn't have any problems. It felt tight, like life was too tight for me. At home, I couldn't move freely. It was like a judge was criticizing our every move. It felt like we were never adequate, never okay, always auditioning for an impossible part.

When she was on the phone, she made it clear that she did not like the person she was talking to either. That was to us anyway, she frowned and acted bored in front of us while sounding sweet to the person she was talking to. Everything was fake. I didn't trust anybody hardly after watching her.

She could fool anybody. She acted proud of that fact. She was manipulative. But she never won because when her act was over, she was sad. She only pretended to be tough. She talked like a victim, crying or mumbling to herself when no adults were around.

Until the mailman came and she perked up. We had a few minutes maybe a few hours when I bought the mail up the hill to her; we would go outside in a hurry before she had a chance to change her mood. Trying to get every last bit of play time in while she went through the mail. We hoped there would be a catalog in there. At any rate, we were out of the house fast.

For a short time I could explore the outdoors, barefoot, wide eyed, and happy. I loved being outdoors. I loved the fresh air, the trees, and the freedom. I kept an eye on my little brother and sister, they were six and seven years younger than me. If they came outside, I did not go past the tree in the side yard, not far from the kitchen door.

When I was about eight or nine, we had an old church bench by the carport that we sat on to play sometimes. It was made of strips of wood that had splinters if you rubbed across them the wrong way. I used to make stick dolls sitting on that bench, with corn silk hair tied on with a piece of an old rag. I always made my doll's hair long because I thought that was important since I was made fun of at home and at school because I had short hair. My Mother called me "bald head" and some of the kids at school called me that too.

Sometimes I would swing on the swing I had made out of a thrown away well rope and a short plank for a seat. It was on a crooked limb of a sturdy plum tree not far from the back door of the house. It was only a few feet off the ground, my feet dragged the dirt when I tried to swing. Most of the time I just sat there and daydreamed. That tree never had any plums but in the spring, it had beautiful white blossoms that smelled like sweet perfume.

It was not far from the burning barrel and later the burning pile because we would throw the trash on the ground next to the barrel and light it on fire. We always burned our trash. I would breathe in the trash smoke as I sat on my swing. But I didn't mind, because I was outside. I could just be, just be for a minute, without running to do something.

3 I HATE MY NAME

"STEPHANIE!" There was my name again. My time was over. Back to work, tending to her every need, trying not to be too hurt by her insults and confusing moods. She seemed to get pleasure in telling us that nobody wanted us around. I hated the sound of my name. She hollered it with such anger and disgust that I did not like to hear it.

It took me a while to separate her madness from my right to be, my right to exist, my right to be respected. I grew into a woman who believed that I was second class at best, worthless as worst.

At every turn, it was an insult.
She said that our granddaddy did not want us living in his house.

"He would rather see me dead than have all these children!" She told me regularly that granddaddy said that to her. I didn't know what to think of my granddaddy. He was always mad too.

My mother said that our aunts were using us as "flunkies" to do stuff for them and we were "too ignorant to know better". She said the same thing about our neighbors, she made sure we knew they didn't like us and that we were fools if we believed they did.

This was a constant thing for her to tell us bad things that people were saying about us. I didn't believe her at first, then I began to wonder if it were true. She had a way of talking that made it seem like she was smart, smarter than anyone else. She convinced me that she knew stuff that no one else did.

But, she was afraid of everybody, even someone else's child. She was intimidated by a child, fearing they would "report back" to their family something about her. "Children aren't anything but tape recorders!" She said. She didn't want any children coming to our house. We only saw other children when it was a birthday party or family gathering. And "You better not tell them anything about my business!" She warned us before we went around anyone. Everything in our house was a secret.

I was amazed at how little she would become on the rare occasions that someone would come by to visit. I knew her to be a strong woman able to move a refrigerator by herself but when it came to another grown-up, especially a man she was dating, she became timid. His needs were more important than hers. I didn't like to see her like that. I wanted her to curse them out like she did us. They didn't seem like they really cared about her. It was like she was there to serve them. They wanted her full attention. They never seemed interested in us. We were sent outside. If it was nighttime, we were left watching TV by ourselves as they went to her bedroom. The men always smoked and drank. I hated their smell of smoke and alcohol mixed with cologne. My mother didn't smoke or drink but we had to get that man, an ash tray. They never married her and moved us into a new house. They never stayed.

When they were gone, she would be back to her old self. Hollering and complaining about us. She would let loose.

It was like her emotions had been bottled up while she pretended to be nice. This was how it always was, we had gotten used to it. I never understood why she was so scared of everybody unless or until she became like a wild animal, fiercely throwing things around, pulling stuff off the wall, picking up whatever she could to hit us. Then and only then would she say how she really felt. She hated everybody. I learned to hate people too. I didn't know I was learning that until I became an adult.

"Don't tell folks your business!"
"What goes on in this house stays in this house!"
"If you tell anybody anything that goes on in this house, I'll beat your ass 'til it rope like okra!" She warned us regularly. And we believed her.

No matter how bad it got at home and how much I wanted to call for help to report her for child abuse, I would not tell anybody. I looked at the phone, then I thought about what she would do to me when they left us at home. Because they, the welfare office or whoever was in charge of helping abused children would not be able to prove that she did anything. Everybody thought she was a nice person.

Besides, I didn't think there was a law against insulting your children and playing mind games on them all the time, or spending all the food stamps the first two weeks of the month and going hungry the rest of the month. I decided it was best to just keep everything to myself. I knew that she would hurt us for telling.

Learning how to pray...

When I was fourteen, I learned how to pray. My aunt, who had graduated from college and lived in Magnolia, had gotten up the nerve to come on Sunday mornings to take us children to church. It was the only place we went except school and the laundromat and the grocery store where we had to be completely silent.

My mother's rage was getting worse. Her beliefs that everybody was talking about her, about us was constant. She told us detailed ways that folks were plotting against us. She told us to fear everybody and that nobody was what they seemed. "The whole world is a stage" She repeated to us. I learned later that that was a famous quote by someone.

I could not trust her, I could not trust people. I began to not trust my own thinking. What was real and what was not, at times I couldn't tell. I just kept doing what I was told. Hoping for relief.

I learned to pray at church. Prayer was a big part of our services. During testimony service, church members would stand up and tell the congregation about the ways their prayers had been answered.

I also remember the big painting of Jesus kneeling on a large rock with a beam of light coming from the sky. He was praying. It hung on the wall at the back of the choir stand. I could see it as I sat out in the congregation, listening to the preacher. I needed something to believe in, something to hold on to.

One day I was feeling bad, I was hurt by the things my mother said to me, I was hurt by the way she tricked us and the look of joy at seeing me hurt. I was scared by her extreme mood swings. I felt hopeless and alone. I felt like I was losing my mind.

That day, my mother had made me heat her bath water in the foot tub to take a bath in the living room like she did often. She had thrown her dirty clothes all over the floor and left her wet towel and bath towel on the floor for me to clean up. Fussing and cursing the whole time, insulting me as usual. She called me ignorant, stupid, ugly, and unwanted, a fool, a flunky, bald head… I never talked back. Even with all that, I had too much respect for her. But I was dying inside.

I was becoming moody. I was mad a lot even though I didn't show it. I didn't like being that way. I felt that I should control my feelings. I believed that I should not be mad at my mother because that was wrong. I had been taught to love and respect my mother. But, I was mad. I was mad at her.

The older I got, the more I could see the mind games she was playing on us. But I was helpless to defend myself. She was strong and violent. She could knock me down with one back hand, one fist.

I tried not to get too close to her when she was raging. I also tried to protect myself mentally, telling myself that she was not telling the truth, that she had her own problems she was dealing with. But she was more cunning than me, than us. We were no match for her lies. And no one came to our rescue. All the grown-ups seemed scared of her.

That particular day, I prayed in a clearing in our pasture. I sat on an old tree stump looking up to heaven. I talked to God.

I asked Him to help me not be angry at my mother. I asked Him to help me not get mad when she called me names or when she was mean to my younger brothers and sister. I asked Him to help me love her regardless of how she treated me. I wanted to be like the saints that we learned about in the bible. I wanted to be longsuffering, patient, and forgiving. After a while, feeling some relief, I went back up to the house.

Nothing changed. It never changed. I did everything that she told me to do plus a little extra trying to lighten her load. I thought that if I could just keep her from feeling stressed, everything would be okay. I forgave her each time she insulted us.

I watched her to learn her moods, I anticipated her angry

outbursts, but even then, there were times that she caught me off guard. She would set us up by being nice or buying us a birthday present. Then as soon as we let down our guard, she would take it back and make fun of us for wanting it. It was a cruel.

I tried not to care about anything. I just went through the motion of living. Like a robot, I did what I was told. I did not smile, I did not laugh. I did not cry. I bottled up my feelings. I survived. We survived. But I was a shell of a person. On the inside I was on the verge of tears every day.

Transferring schools...

By then we had transferred to Emerson School from Walker. I was in the tenth grade. From my first year until I graduated, I went to school every day, I made good grades, and I was well behaved. I received many awards, distinctions, and opportunities. I was named most likely to succeed in my yearbook. I was chosen Miss Emerson High School. During my senior year, I was crowned Homecoming Queen. The night I was crowned was the most special night of my life. I felt valued. I felt pretty. I felt appreciated. All the things I had not experienced with my mother.

I still wonder how I made it through each day. How I managed to keep a positive attitude. I now believe that God did answer my prayer that day. He made me stronger.

I was active in school organizations, mostly those I could participate in during the school day. My mother refused to give us a ride to any events. If I did have to stay after school, I did so in fear of her attacks when I got home.

Sometimes, a kind teacher or one of my aunts would give me a ride home. I was always distracted, not fully focused, I worried a lot. My mother's negative words threatening to suffocate my every thought.

She never acknowledged any of my accomplishments. Every good thing was trampled with insults and conspiracies. I learned to dream in silence. Even then, I half believed that I was not worth my dreams, that I had no right to them.

During my last semester of high school, I started to slip farther and farther from any positive view of myself. Even though I was doing well in my school work and my church work, I felt sad and overly self-conscious.

I struggled not to think negatively. The bus ride home from school was my time to close the door to possibilities and put on the armor I needed to withstand my mother's behavior. I was falling apart internally.

At church I did everything that was asked of me. I was the Sunday school secretary, reading the minutes before the congregation. I was in the choir. I watched my younger brothers and sister when we were at church, I ushered along with other teenagers my age, and I was on every youth program speaking or reading something. I looked forward to church.

But, every Saturday night and Sunday morning, my mother ridiculed us for going to church. She hated church folks. The only prayer she ever said was "Jesus wept" before she took her food back to her bedroom to eat. She said all the people at church were hypocrites, that it did not take all that going to church to be "saved". She said that they were ignorant with "all that jumping and shouting!" Sometimes she'd shuffle her feet as if to mimic them shouting. Shouting was excited, spirit-filled dancing. We went to a sanctified church.

This was the church she had been raised in but, she hated it. The building was different and in a different location but the congregation was basically the same folks. She told me that when she was a teenager, her mother had had a stroke and nobody from the church came to see them after the initial visits. She said that no one cared and that the only thing that mattered to them was "going to church".

She said "church was more than going to a building." She didn't go except on Easter Sunday and maybe Homecoming. She told us that it did not do any good for us to go every Sunday. It was a struggle for me to keep going. My aunt would drive from Magnolia to Emerson, pick us up, take us to the small country church where she was also a member, then bring us back home. The house would be cold, bath water still in the foot tub in the middle of the floor as we had rushed to be ready on time. My aunt went back to Magnolia. I turned on the gas heaters to warm the house.

I reminded my brothers and sister to change out of their church clothes so they could wear them again. I straightened up the house and went into the kitchen to find something to eat. During those years, I cooked a lot of cornbread or baked biscuits from a can, and boiled sugar and water to make sugar syrup to eat with it. If there was a whole chicken in the deep freezer, I took it out the night before. After church, I cut it up and fried it. That was on a good day.

Most Sundays my mother was working at the nursing home when we got home from church. By the time she got there, the house was in order and all the children were fed. When I heard her pull up, I fixed her plate just like she had told me to. It was supposed to be ready when she came in. She changed out of her uniform and got comfortable in her house dress. I took her plate to her in the living room. It was always an ordeal as she complained "This chicken is too damn hard!" She said chicken was supposed to be fried so that it came out "soft".

As soon as she had everything she needed, it was time for me to do homework and get clothes out for all of us for school, except for my brother who was only two years younger than me. He got out his own clothes. If I didn't get the clothes out the night before, we would miss the bus and have to stay home all day. My mother would not think of taking us to school if we missed the bus. Most days she was already gone to work anyway.

My mother's children were more like my children. I stopped looking for her to help us because she wouldn't. She made it known that we were on our own. She paid the bills and that was it. Food was not a right, it was privilege. She made us feel guilty for needing to eat. Like it was always a bother to provide for us.

My personal hygiene was a subject for ridicule and deprivation. She would not buy me what I needed for my menstrual cycle, instead throwing a bag of large hospital size maxi pads at me. I had bad cramps, but she taught me nothing. I learned on my own. I'm grateful for what I had learned in home economics class, from the educational films on development. At least I knew what was happening the first time it happened.

She called me names. Hurting physically and being insulted at the same time was a terrible pain for me. It was more than I could take. I remember feeling like I was becoming dizzy, my thoughts swirling around in my head. I was trying to keep my focus. I was losing contact with myself.

She was more intense when I was hurting, it was like her rage was increased. Like my normal development was infuriating to her. She was suspicious of something, that I was becoming something that was nasty. She made reference to sexual behavior, like I was becoming sexually active. I wasn't. I hadn't. That was not a thought for me at that time. I was just trying to make it from day to day. She made comments about me that I did not understand but saw the anger in her face. She made me feel dirty, like I should be ashamed of my body, my growing up. I loved her but I knew she was dangerous. She was dangerous to my mind.

4 HER TRASH CANS

It was like she would dump all of her animosity for the world on us. There was no rest for me, no off days from her rage. What was real? We never knew. There were two or three hours at a time it seemed, before she remembered a word or look or an insult from her past or a hardship, or having been a victim of something. She had a lot of memories of being a victim of different things and she expressed her sadness and anger.

It was as though she didn't think she deserved to be happy, that the world was a hard place and even family members could not be trusted.

There were sporadic moments when she looked happy but they came and went quickly. During those times she would clean the house while we were at school or sleeping. She washed the dishes including the ones she had used days before that still had the crumbs stuck to them. If it was while we were at school, we would get off the bus, and when we got to the porch, smell pinto beans and fried chicken.

If she was really feeling good, she would have the big yellow pot full of thick cut rounds of sweet potatoes in thick syrupy juice. Then she would smile and maybe even laugh. But the sadness soon returned. She would go back to her bedroom. Mad at the world. Mad and sad.

The days she cooked were like from heaven. The house was spotlessly cleaned and she would be sitting on the couch in her flowered house dress, full figured, hair combed, like a woman in the home and garden magazines. The smell of Mr. Clean and Old English furniture polish was in the air. And for a moment she acted like she liked us.

Those days I sill cherish. Those days are the ones that gave me hope to keep doing what she told us and maybe those days would last.

"You all better get something," she would say, as she sat on the couch with her plate on the newly polished coffee table. The food was hot on the stove. My younger siblings went to change out of their school clothes. In the kitchen, a quick look at the stove and I would divide up the food in my head. I thought of how much each person could get so that it was enough for all of us children. I fixed my little brother and sister's plates, spreading it so it cooled before they started eating. My other brother, I fixed his plate too because, if I didn't he would eat more than his share.

Once the food was divided and there was some left, if he ate more that was up to him. We ate at the kitchen table. It was my job to wash the dishes and clean the kitchen. I made sure everybody did their homework and laid everybody's clothes out for the next day, my usual routine. Except for my brother next to me. He didn't care about clothes. He might sleep in his clothes and wear them again the next day if he felt like it. He didn't follow many rules. After a while, my mother stopped giving him any and made me do his work. She would say it was no hope for him. That he was lazy and there was something wrong with him. That was her way of trying to control him mentally since she was losing physical control.

"You have to leave a fool alone" she'd say to me like she always did, then make me do all the work. He didn't care much about anybody else. He did crank the truck for her on cold days then get back in his bed fully dressed until it was time to go to school. He got away with a lot until he was in about in the tenth grade and he started to care about how he looked. I knew this from photos that I saw back home after I had moved away. He had become a handsome young man, responsible, and hardworking.

I think when he was growing up, he was developing his own personality, and his hardness may have been his way of coping, of surviving.

He has looked out for my mother since his first part-time job in high school. We both learned how to make it on our own, trying to reassemble our childhood and her madness that continues, into something that we can live with. Even as adults, we have to watch our hearts, protect our peace, and love our mother at the same time. It's more than forgiveness, it's the grace to continue to engage and help her when every effort you make is twisted against you.

My little sister...

My little sister was very mild mannered. She didn't talk much and when she did it was soft spoken. She cried a lot. Not out loud, but a quiet cry. Sometimes, she would just have tears in her eyes. She was sick a lot with asthma and bronchitis. I was responsible for taking care of her. If she got really bad my mother took her to the doctor on her Medicaid card. My mother acted like this was an inconvenience for her.

If my sister was sick on a school day and she had to go to work, my mother would make me miss school to care for her. I hated missing school but I didn't mind looking out for my sister.

I was in the fifth grade, at Walker, when my mother first started making me miss school to help out around the house, but back then she was not working, with two toddlers at home. She would make me stay home to "get in wood" for the wood heater and do other chores.

As a teenager, I still hated to miss school. But, I loved my little sister. She was precious to me. I kept up with her Primatene Mist inhaler and her prescriptions from the doctor. I kept the humidifier filled with water and with a little Vicks Vapor-rub in it, near our bed. I watched her to make sure she didn't get too hot or too cold. She would be so weak when she got sick. It broke my heart to see her like that. She eventually grew out of it.

On cold nights, I made sure the bedroom that she and I shared was warm, putting a towel under the door to keep the draft out, and the heavy quilt on our bed. We had to turn the gas heater down so low, we barely felt the heat. The house was freezing cold, sometimes the linoleum rugs cracked. When the temperature outside dropped below freezing, icicles formed on the inside of our windowsills.

My mother said that the house was so cold because my granddaddy did not finish it so the floors did not have anything to stop the cold wind from coming through.

She said that the house was freezing inside because there was no insulation in the walls. She said he did a poor job with that house. It was a United Built home that he had built in the 1970's. It had three small bedrooms, a living room, kitchen, a tiny bathroom, and two very small closets. The sink in the bathroom was not on a cabinet. I was just the face bowl that hung on the wall and fell off the wall if you bumped it. We seldom were able to use the bathtub because we didn't have enough running water.

The house was white with yellow shutters, a gray painted porch and cement steps. Inside, there were places where you could see the two-by-fours and electrical wires. It was freezing cold in the winters and too hot in the summer.

There was a gas heater in each room that we had to stand close to so we could feel the heat. There was no air conditioning. It sat out in the open with no shade. The sun beaming down on it in the summers. The well was low, it had not been dug deep enough to provide regular and clean running water. But, I loved that house because it was not the barn that we had moved from. No cows had walked through it, hay had not been stored in the rafters. My mother had moved us into what had been the home I was born in but, had been turned into a barn.

We, my mother, my brother and I, cleaned it out and pulled up part of the manure stained floor, replaced it with plywood, patched up the broken windows, and added a wood heater. My mother had my brother and I climb a ladder to patch the leaks in the tin roof with hot tar. It had no running water at all. That was where we had lived just before moving back into the United Built house which things unfinished but, at least it was a real house.

My mother complained constantly. She complained about everything my granddaddy did. Our toilet stopped up all the time. Many days we had to pour water in the tank to make it flush, not all the way full because we had to save water. If the sewage line got backed up, we had to wait for granddaddy to come by with the long spring like thing he used to push through at the end of the plastic pipe that ran from our bathroom to the open sewage down the hill. That's how he unclogged the sewage pipe. It was a terrible site to see the sewage like a large puddle on the ground with nowhere to go. Even then, that didn't make sense to me. My granddaddy fussed and cursed, blaming us for the stopped up pipe. I think now that there was nowhere for the sewage to go so it piled up in that spot. That maybe the drainage was not finished or not done correctly when the house was built. The problems with the lines were not our fault but, he made us think it was.

He talked about us like we were not there saying how "Wursome", his way of saying worrisome, that we were.

Anytime he had to come to the house to make a repair, if my mother could not do it herself, he was annoyed, fussing and cursing the whole time.

"These damn children will tear up anything!" He said. "Wear the devil out of me!" He said looking aggravated, frowning, walking fast. He always walked fast, talking the whole time, annoyed. But it wasn't just with us, he was annoyed with everybody. He talked about all of his children like he was frustrated with them about something or another. They never seemed to do anything right.

My mother used to panic if she heard his truck coming up the road.

We could tell from way up the road through an opening in the trees when granddaddy's truck was coming. A big orange dust cloud behind him as he sped up the dirt road to our house. My mother would get nervous, running around telling us to "Clean up!", and "Move this or hide that mail!" She was always hiding something from granddaddy. She didn't want him to see the bills for the furniture or clothes she had bought that she couldn't afford. She was scared of his opinion of her. She even acted like she did not like it when he talked about us. Like it hurt her, even though she said worse.

When he was gone, she would use what he said about us against us. "That's why he doesn't want you around, you all tear up everything!" Then came her famous saying, "He said he would rather see me dead than with all these children." She was sad when she said that, looking off in the distance like she was staring into an empty place. It was a while after he left before she came back to herself. She would just sit there. I felt bad for her. Then she would go to her bedroom and stay a long time. Sometimes later I would hear her mumbling something to herself. Sometimes crying.

Our house was always a mess. It wasn't because I didn't

pick up after her but, she kept throwing things on the floor, on the dresser tops, kicking stuff under her bed, throwing her Ambi or foundation here or there, or putting her dentures on top of the television in a cup from the kitchen. She had a case for them, but she wouldn't use it. We never knew when we might see her dentures in a cup we normally used. It was like the more extreme it seemed, the more she would do it to see us react, to see us puzzled, or grossed out. Then call us crazy if we looked confused by what she did. It was a weird game she played.

One day she got mad about the hot water heater that was not working right and in a fit of rage, picked it up and threw it out the back door. She had no plan of how to get another one. That was another argument with her and granddaddy. He fixed what needed to be fixed if only partly or temporarily. He was impatient and liked to cut corners. He never seemed to care about the long term. Just enough to get by in that moment.

My mother said she hated that about him. But, she made few attempts to do better, to get out from under his provision. He paid the house note and provided her a truck for transportation. She ran up bills in his name that she couldn't pay. She used the money she made from work to pay the light bill, buy a few groceries when the food stamps ran out, the household supplies, and gas for the truck. Once I saw her check stub, she made about $5000.00 a year for full-time work as a nurse's assistant at the nursing home.

She paid her bills, if she had to pay a little at a time. She had one bad habit though, she liked expensive things, things of good quality. She bought things that would last a long time and they usually cost more. She stressed about how to pay for them. "It's about quality," she would say. We had the newest fancy refrigerator that we had to clean a certain way so that the empty shelves looked just right. "Use vinegar and water", she said, "that's all you need!"

The washing machine was state of the art with a

"Delicate" cycle for her uniforms. She was serious about her uniforms. She kept them white. She wore them well. She'd washed them on the delicate cycle and put them on a hanger on a nail on the front porch to air dry. But we hardly ever had enough water in our shallow well to make the washing machine work.

We still had to go to the laundromat. Many times she washed her uniforms by hand in a pan of water then hung them up to dry.

She taught me early how to care for her uniforms. Then it became my responsibility to make sure she had a clean, ironed uniform each day she went to work. Laying her clothes out was a requirement before I could go to bed. Everything she needed: her uniform, slip, underclothes, white stockings, freshly polished nursing shoes, and hand washed and bleached white shoestrings, had to be laid out.

All of the personal supplies she needed and her Avon perfume, foundation and rouge, comb, Ambi face brightening cream, Ultra Sheen hair grease, and Royal Crown for her legs, had to be right where she could reach them as she needed them. She only wore a little foundation and dab of rouge, saying that anything more would make a woman look like a street walker. She told me never to wear any. Lipstick was definitely out of the question. She even hated to see women with color in their hair except black, like she used.

Then that morning I had to be on hand to assist her getting dressed. Passing her what she needed. I could not get dressed until she had pulled out of the driveway on her way to work. Then I woke up my siblings and started my morning routine. It was that way every day that she went to work. When she got home, she threw her things everywhere. It was my job to keep up with them.

She bought clothes that were expensive and made of high quality fabrics from the highest priced stores in Magnolia. Not a lot of clothes, just what she needed for the one or two times she went to church a year, a funeral when she had to go to one, and nice comfortable clothes to wear to town. She was conscious of how she looked at all times when she went somewhere. She thought you could tell a lot about a person by the quality of fabric of their clothes.

She bragged that she had a "charge account" and that she could buy anything she wanted. Then she would take the clothes back without ever wearing them when she needed the money back, which was almost all the time. It was like for a moment she could feel like she had something. She hated being poor.

She ran up bills in my granddaddy's name at Montgomery Wards, Sears, and charged things at Western Auto. It was a constant argument with them. She'd cry about it, get mad, say she deserved nice things, that granddaddy did not know better, over and over, month after month, sneaking behind his back, getting caught, arguing. He talked about her so bad, like she was the worst thing on earth. It was hard to watch them, to hear them. They looked so angry at each other, they both had strong language and they argued with intensity. I tried to distract myself and the other children but they were so loud I couldn't. They're arguing made me feel uneasy.

5 LOOKING THE PART

We were clean and we dressed well, using what we had the best we could. We had good manners and followed instructions well. On the outside, we looked like we were okay. On the inside, we were also often stressed, walking a tight rope to keep our home life separate from school or church.

Though everybody who knew my family knew we were raised by my mother alone, she did not let us look like we were missing anything. No matter how hard it got, we acted like everything was fine.

We never ate a whole chicken, I would put a piece or two back to divide between us at the next meal. I could cut one chicken breast into six small pieces. We'd have one piece of chicken a piece for each meal. But most days we ate cornflakes and milk. When the whole milk was gone, we used PET milk, when it was gone, we used water in our cereal.

When the younger children were babies and preschoolers, my mother could get WIC vouchers for free cereal, milk, eggs, cheese, and fruit juice. The vouchers only allowed for cereal like cornflakes, Special K, Total, and other unsweetened cereal. When my siblings got older, she bought food with food stamps. If she worked extra days, her food stamps would be cut. She said that she couldn't win. If she worked, she received less aid. She always qualified for something.

When we were younger, she took us all with her to the welfare office. She had to recertify for benefits every few months. Back then she did not have a job, she was getting a small welfare check every month. Because she didn't have a vehicle, she'd catch a ride with someone, paying them a few dollars for their trouble. We'd all load into their car.

They were on their way to work in Magnolia, so we stayed at the welfare office all day until they got off. It was my mother and four children. She'd have the large diaper bag full of milk and diapers for the babies and snacks for us older children. We also had our appointments at the county health office that same day. All the children would get checkups and immunizations and the she could requalify for WIC for the little ones.

She tried to have all of her appointments on the same day so she didn't have to bother anyone for a ride. She thought no one wanted to be bothered with her and all of us so she asked for help or a ride only when she had to.

 She would have to get her recertification forms signed for her welfare check and food stamps by someone outside of her household, to verify that she had no income at that time. She'd take that form with all the others she had to fill out quarterly or so. She always seemed nervous that she would not be able to get benefits for some reason or another.

She hated that someone outside her house had to know she was on welfare. She felt that was an invasion of her privacy. Later, a van would come to pick the children up for medical and dental appointments. We took the long ride to Magnolia in a van with a nice woman driving. That was before my mother started working at the nursing home.

By then, I was thirteen, and she didn't get a welfare

check anymore, just food stamps. They came in a brown envelope at the first of the month. We really liked to see the sixty-five dollar booklet of food stamps. We got about one hundred and fifty dollars in total. We got more when she did not have a job.

I was so glad to see the mailman put that envelope in our mailbox.

Toys from the dump...

We didn't overeat, trying to save something for later, and we were active. My granddaddy would bring us toys from the town dump. He'd back up the truck and start throwing junk in the yard for us to go through. He always had some old toys in there. My mother would get mad, saying we were going to get "Legionnaires" disease from that dirty stuff. She never said it out loud to granddaddy. She just made us feel bad for wanting the toys he threw in our yard. Most of them were in pretty good shape.

We wiped the dirt off and if a wheel or part was missing, we didn't complain. We were happy to have it. He would bring old bicycles that had no tires, just rims and the chains falling off. My brother and I learned to put the chains on and ride the bikes on their rims. We'd push them up a hill and roll down, rolling fast, using our feet to stop.

My uncle bought me my first bike, it was a purple Huffy. It was beautiful. I just looked at it, not wanting to ride it because I did not know how to ride a bike with tires, and brakes, or one that was not a raggedy piece of junk. I eventually did and I loved it. That was the only bike I ever got, I rode it until it until I got too big for it.

We watched a lot of television. After we ate dinner on school days, it was the after school specials on ABC, one of the three channels that we had. We had an old floor model TV and my mother ran an antenna wire through the living room window to the metal antenna on the roof. We'd move the wire around to get a good reception. If that didn't work, we'd climb the ladder and turn it until the "picture was clear".

The after school specials were good shows that taught us something about friendship, family, or some other good thing we didn't see except on television. They showed families in clean houses, sitting around the dinner table, and a mother and a father who loved each other and their children.

Then it was Scooby Doo or Tom & Jerry before going outside until the news went off, if it was not wintertime.

We stayed in the house if it was winter, everybody in the living room because the other rooms were too cold. My mother would not let us play outside in the wintertime, even the days it wasn't that cold.

On cold days, especially when it was ice on the ground, we slept in one room. One winter, the roads were iced over, no one could get in or out of our area. We ran out of butane, we had no heat. We slept on a mattress that my mother put in the middle of the living room floor. All the children slept on the mattress with two or three quilts to keep warm, and she slept on the couch. We cooked rice in a crock pot in the living room and added government butter and cheese to it to make a meal. That was some of the best rice.

Typical days…

We did our homework with the TV on. That was one thing we could do, we could watch TV every day for hours at a time. It was our only entertainment when we were inside. It was my mother's escape, she talked about all the things she would have, like the people did on TV, if her life were different. It was on until 10:00pm. Then we knew to turn off everything and go to bed. Some nights my mother was up watching TV with us, talking through the shows.

Sometimes she would laugh and then we laughed, just a little. We didn't dare laugh too much. Most nights she would leave us in the living room by ourselves and go to her bedroom, close the door and not say anything to us the rest of the night. We knew what we were supposed to do and we did it. We turned everything off at 10:00pm and went to bed. We were on our own on in the mornings.

She would holler for me to wake up. She always hollered at me in the mornings. At 6:00am I was up helping her get dressed for work. "Get me my long lined bra!" or "Hand me my slip!", and I was expected to hand it to her promptly. I put the shoestrings that I had washed the night before and hung on a chair to dry, in her shoes while she put her clothes on.

I knew that when she got the white stockings on that I had better have the shoestrings in and the shoe tongue pulled back. I was to hold each shoe steady so she could easily put her foot in each one. If anything was not done just right she would get mad. Even when everything went like clockwork, she would act like she couldn't put her foot in the shoe, moving her foot aggressively and complaining while fussing at me to tie her shoe. I could tell she was making it more difficult for me to help her put her shoes on. I just did not understand why.

"Tie my damn shoe!" She said in anger.
"You can't do anything right!" "Damn fool!" She'd scream in anger, kicking her foot at me like I was in her way.

When she was really aggravated, she'd reach down and grab me by my head scarf and hair and sling me to the floor or hit me across my back. She'd be in such a rage. If her shoe was still untied, she'd threaten me to do it again.

"I'll beat your ass if you don't tie my shoe!" That was how she did it, she'd make it almost impossible to follow her directions then lash out at us for not doing what she said.

I was scared trying to tie her shoes, trying to keep my eye on her and dodge her attacks. I was also starting to feel anger towards her. This happened every morning that she went to work. The same routine.

She was not just mad at me, she talked about her supervisor and some of the folks she worked with. She said she could run the place better than her supervisor could. She would go over things that happened the day before, she was still mad.

Many times she had to go in on her off days. They would call her to fill in for somebody. She'd be tired and trying to get some sleep when they called. When the phone rang at 7:00am, she would get nervous.

Sometimes she wouldn't answer the phone. Somebody was always calling in sick at her job. She never called in sick and never said no when they told her to come in on her off day but she made us pay for it. She wouldn't stand up for herself with grown-ups. She felt if she said no she would lose her job. She told us everything she wanted to say to them. She went to work mad. But I know now that she became a sweet lady once she got there.

It was the early 1980's. A few times I went to work with her for some reason or another. Once she showed me a plaque where she was the employee of the month. I couldn't believe it. All the patients loved her. The other nurse's aides loved her. It was like she walked on air in her cushioned nursing shoes that I had polished and tied up before she came to work. She was nothing like she was at home.

She did her work with ease and talked in a way I had never heard her talk before, light and with a sense of humor. She looked comfortable with her work. The aides worked together in harmony. My mother looked professional and kind. I didn't know that person I was seeing but, I liked her. I wished she could stay that way. I was saddened knowing that it would not last. I went back to the lobby and read magazine after magazine, until it was

3:00pm and my mother's shift was over. It was a Saturday, I still don't remember why she took me with her or who kept my brothers and sister that day.

On school days, my brother would "crank the truck" for her if it was cold outside. At 6:30am she was backing the truck out of the carport on her way to Magnolia to do her shift. I breathed a little easier. Then it was time to get the littles ones up, faces washed and teeth brushed, hair combed, and dressed for school.

We never ate breakfast before school. We ate free breakfast and free lunch there. When we were at Walker school, we were only given a carton of milk in the mornings but I looked forward to that small carton of white milk. I didn't like the chocolate milk.

My favorite was the free lunch. The ladies in the cafeteria were great cooks. They made everything taste good and it was always hot like they just took it off the stove. I could see the kitchen when I picked up my tray, it was clean and the ladies were neat. They stood in a row fixing trays making small talk with some of the students as they came through the line. The room was not very big with long tables connected into two or three long rows. The whole room smelled like the kitchen of somebody's house who thought you were special. Someone who was cooking just for you.

After we transferred to Emerson school, I didn't know anybody there except my cousins who lived in that town. The cafeteria was huge. The kitchen was stainless steel, all I could see was shiny silver countertops and appliances. The ladies were in a row fixing trays just like my old school. But, they didn't seem to know the kids like at my old school. They knew them but it was different. At Walker, they knew my whole family and my grandparents. That was good and bad, because any teacher or lunch lady could see your folks and tell them how you were acting at school.

As I went through the line at Emerson, I didn't talk much. I was surprised when the food was good. Almost as good as my old school. We had free breakfast too. The mini cinnamon rolls or the sausage and biscuits were my favorites. I thought of my little brother and sister in elementary school and was glad that they would have food to eat too. Then I only had to worry about our dinner. I decided to not think about it until my bus ride home. Until then, I could just enjoy school.

Emerson school had large halls with glossy floors and large classrooms. We had all sorts of equipment in gym class. I learned to play all kinds of sports. I had a great gym teacher, a white male, who was tall and kind. He was also the basketball coach. Years later he would be the one who talked my mother into letting my brother play basketball, volunteering to give him a ride home after practice. Before that my mother would not let him participate even though he loved basketball and played for hours on the dirt with a bike rim he'd nailed to a tall pole for a goal. My brother became a star player. It was that that allowed him to go to a community college after graduation. From there to a four year college.

Starting to blame myself...

I liked school and dreaded the end of the school day. At home, I was grateful for the quiet days here and there. Those were the days that gave me sanity. But a strange thing happened.

I started blaming myself for causing my mother to treat me badly. I was her target, the others escaped with less damage. She insulted all of us but me in particular. Everything I did was wrong. She seemed to have felt a certain satisfaction in hurting me, in disappointing me by getting my hopes up about something then pulling it away.

"Po fool", she would say. She'd dragged it out. "P-o F-o-o-l" as if she couldn't believe how naive I was as she sat on the couch after she'd told me an unbelievable story about some plot against me. By then I was more amazed at the length she'd go to hurt us than the lie she was telling. She was a good liar. She had a creative imagination.

I tried hard not to hope or expect anything from her, but sometimes I would fall into hoping or anticipate a trip to Magnolia or she would say she was going to buy us something that we needed, a small thing. Then almost like it made her tired to think about it, she pulled the idea away, and didn't do what she had said she would. Then she acted aggravated that we had even wanted it. I never hoped for anything big because I knew we didn't have the money.

I started picking collard greens for five dollars for my aunt's in-laws who sold vegetables to a store in Magnolia. Later, I cleaned the house of the woman my mother used to ride to work with to make money.

I got my first part-time job when I was sixteen. I worked a few hours a week in a program for low income students. I think it was called JTPA then. I received a small stipend. I used the money to buy personal supplies for me and my siblings. One Easter, I bought a little white straw hat with a pink ribbon for my little sister to wear to church. I worked part-time until I graduated from high school.

It was a blessing for me to be chosen for Upward Bound. I could not believe that I received twenty dollars every two weeks to learn.

I loved going to the college after school on Upward Bound days. I prepared the night before for my siblings. I gave them directions on what was there to eat and other things they needed since I would not be there. I worried about them.

The Upward Bound drivers picked us up at our schools and drove us to the Southern Arkansas University campus in Magnolia. The cafeteria was the largest I had seen except for the school field trip to Henderson University for an FBLA conference.

At the SAU cafeteria, there was so much food. So many different kinds of food and all I had to do was choose what I wanted. I hadn't had that much freedom before. I couldn't believe that people lived like that, so few restrictions, so many options.

Then there were the classes that we attended. English, Math, and more. I met students from all over South Arkansas. It was a joy. After the classes, the drivers took us to our homes. I was the last one in our car or van, to be dropped off. The drivers were driving and looking like they were going to the end of the earth as they drove to my house.

It was pitch black, the road was orange dirt, flanked by trees. The road narrowed near the bridge over the small creek as if we were coming to a dead end, only one car could go across at a time. Then we passed through the "bottom" as the low lying area was called. On one side of the road was a small pond where my aunts and grown cousins used to go "muddying", using a hoe to push the mud at the bottom back and forth to reveal the catfish they'd then catch with their hands or a net.

When it rained hard, that spot would fill up and overflow over the road until the road could not be seen. It would look like a lake. If the rain was not as hard, the road would become an orange muddy mess that vehicles got stuck in regularly. They would have to walk to our house to call someone with a pulpwood truck to pull them out. That was just below where we lived.

As we rode through the darkness, with only the light from our headlights, it was like I was seeing it for the first time. It was the first time that I was with people who did not know about the area. It was like I had a fresh perspective. I had not been allowed to go anywhere on my own. I missed my siblings and thought of them many times when I was away, looking forward to seeing them when I got home. Sometimes they were up when I got there. My mother would be in bed.

I assured the driver that we were going the right way. I began to feel bad that I lived so far out.

6 MIND GAMES

Some summer days my mother would make us all get dressed and ready to go to this or that place, usually to Magnolia. Once when they had just built the McDonalds in town, my mother told us that she was going to take us there. It was the early 1980's. That was before I got wise to her behavior.

For hours we were getting dressed, changing a shirt or pair of pants over and over to fit her idea of what we should look like. Then she might hand wash a different blouse in the middle of all this, lay it on a towel, roll it up, squeeze it to get the excess water out, then tell me to hang it on the porch.

We'd be sitting on the couch all dressed waiting for her to decide if we were going anywhere. Sometimes for hours. Trying to be still, trying not to aggravate her. She told us to sit there so we didn't mess up our clothes until she was ready to go. She might change her clothes four times, standing in front the full-length of square mirrors that were stuck on the living room wall. If she needed something, she'd tell me to get it for her. I had lined up her cosmetics and perfume on the top of the old floor model TV that she used as her dressing table. She'd stand there combing her hair and brushing down her edges, maybe pinning on her hair piece, dissatisfied about how she looked.

She'd talk the whole time about how she couldn't do the things she wanted to do. How frustrated she was. Sometimes looking sad, sometimes angry. She'd relive conversations with people. She'd turn this way then that way to see herself from different angles. The house was so hot that she would be pouring with sweat, her curls would fall flat. As the hours wore on, she'd go from excited about the possibility of a trip to town, to exhaustion.

It was grueling. Because about the second hour of sitting there, waiting, we knew we were not going anywhere.

After about the third time of her doing this over the course of a summer, we knew what to expect. But we also knew that we had to go along with her or she'd hit us with something. Disobeying her was not something that we thought about.

She was always saying she didn't have the "right clothes", that her "hair needed to be done", or that "These nasty ass children" were the reason she couldn't go anywhere when she wanted to. She always sounded trap. Like she had no choices.

She blamed us for everything that was wrong in her life. I felt useless and unwanted. That was the spirit I carried with me all day almost every day. Even though I knew what she was doing and saying did not make sense, it still affected me.

When I was reading, I felt better. I could imagine all the interesting things I was reading about. I wanted to be reading as I was sitting there waiting for an imaginary trip to town. But, she had to have our full attention. I sat there waiting for the show to be over and we could get out of those hot clothes and back to our day around the house.

By the end, she would be flustered saying, "Forget it, it's no use." Then she'd change into her house dress.

Disappointed but relieved, we changed too. I hated it for my little brother and sister the most.

A memory...The night she cut off my hair...

"STEPHANIE!" "Get up and get me the scissors." "You need to cut that mess off your head." She yelled.
She woke me up in the middle of the night to cut my hair off.
"Your hair sticking out looking crazy, it needs to be cut off and shaped up!"
"You need a more natural, clean cut even look." She said as if she was offended by my hair.
She made me sit down on the floor between her knees and threw the paper rollers out of my hair onto the floor fussing the whole time about how bad my hair looked. I was in the seventh grade.

She used the big heavy scissors that she used to cut fabric when she was making a dress. They were dull or felt that way to me as I heard her cutting off two inches of my beloved three inch hair. I had learned to wear it down, no pony tails, or in my case, not the three ponytails I had worn every day from first through fifth grades. She made me wear it like that every single day; one short ponytail on top and two tiny ones at the back on each side near the back of my neck.

Then one day out of the blue she told me I was getting a curl. It was the summer after the fifth grade. She had saved or more likely didn't pay something else to get me an expensive Jheri Curl. It was a popular and expensive hair treatment that many black people were wearing at the time.

It was considered fashionable to have a curl in the 1970s and later in the 1980's. I was surprised my mother had decided to get me one. We had never talked about it. Although I liked them on other people, I never thought about getting one, besides, I knew we couldn't afford it.

Like a lot of times when my mother had an idea, an impulse, nothing stopped her. I had no choice but to go along with her, she was in charge. Children had no rights as far as she was concerned.

I also knew that as quickly as she decided to do something, she could change her mind halfway through it. Then leave me in a tough situation.

She took me to her beautician. It took all day between getting the loud smelling chemicals on my hair down to my scalp to straighten it out, then rolling it in small sections with tiny hard plastic rollers with an elastic rubber tip to hold them in place. After that, all of my hair was drenched with some liquid. With my head full of rollers and covered with a plastic cap, I was put under the dryer for hours.

I didn't mind though because I knew my hair would be straight and curly when it was all done.

Finally, it was finished. I walked out of the beauty shop feeling good. But that didn't last long. My mother's anger came back. She was probably mad about all the money she had spent to get my hair done. That was the tough part about her spontaneous decisions, the letdown afterwards. Her regrets, her blaming, her criticizing, her insults. She took her frustration about herself out on me. I could tell when we left the beauty shop that it was coming.

She bought me one or two bottles of curl activator that was required to keep up the curl. Each time making me feel bad for needing it. She didn't buy me anymore. I was on my own when it ran out.

After several months of sparingly squeezing out the curl activator, I ran out. My curl was getting old. My mother would not even mention me getting a refresher or any upkeep. Month after month went by with my hair becoming more nappy. It only looked halfway good if I put water on it.

One day I remembered how curly my hair looked with the conditioner after it was washed. I loaded my hair with conditioner one morning as I was getting dressed for school. I was in the sixth grade. My curls sprung back, at least on the ends. It looked kind of good. I patted it into a nice shape. Off to catch the bus, so far so good. But, before lunch it was drying up.

By the afternoon it was hard, packed to my head and a cloudy white color because the conditioner had dried up. It looked worse than before. From that I learned that conditioner is no substitute for curl activator. I had been desperate and my mother would not help me. So I tried to do something myself. It didn't work out at all like I hoped.

When I got home, I wiped the conditioner out with a wet towel. I think an aunt bought me some curl activator. Eventually my mother washed and pressed my hair. I learned to roll it at night when she had gone to bed and my sister and brothers were also in bed and I had some time for myself. I'd roll my hair with torn pieces of a paper bag that I twisted my hair around.

I did this in the dark because we were not allowed to have any lights on after 10:00pm. The next morning after I had assisted my mother getting ready for work, I would take the paper rollers out and comb my hair into a reasonable style. My mother hated that. It was not good enough.

It was on one of those nights after I had rolled my hair, put my scarf on, and went to sleep, that my mother yelled for me to get up. She wanted to cut my hair.

I couldn't believe it. I was deeply hurt.

Calling me names, insulting my hair combing skills, putting me down and her favorite, "they".

"They think you look stupid with your ends sticking out in a so called wearing your hair down!" She said, making fun of me.

Then after cutting my hair off to about 1 inch, to the new growth, she was disappointed at how it turned out.

Even though she would not take me to get upkeep or buy me the supplies I needed to maintain the curl I had gotten over a year ago, she was blaming me. I felt helpless.

Knowing she was wrong or at least feeling that way, I still had too much respect to disobey her. I sat there on the floor as she cut and cursed until almost all my hair was gone. Then dissatisfied about how it looked she dismissed me to clean up the hair that was all over the floor, and go back to bed. No explanation. No instructions on upkeep. No encouragement.

Just dismissed as if I was nothing. I felt like there was no use trying to take care of myself. Like everything that I tried to do that was good for me, she tried to destroy.

Humiliated at school...

The next morning, still feeling bad, and with a broken heart, I did all my chores as usual, and got ready for school.

The day before I had gone to school proud of my hair styling, and I was making improvements each day. Then suddenly I was embarrassed again with no support from my mother who by that morning was laughing at me. I could not make it look right so I put on an old sweater cap with decorative suede patches around the head part and yarn around the brim. I put it on even though it was barely cold enough for a jacket let alone a hat made of yarn and suede I wore it all day at school.

I was going to school at Walker. I'd almost made it through the day when my English teacher called me out. I was sitting at my desk preparing to do my work. She walked over to my desk and asked,

"Why are you wearing that hat in my class?" She spoke as if I knew better than to disrespect her classroom by wearing a hat inside.

"Take that it off!"

I slowly removed my hat.

Then she said in a loud voice,

"Why did you get your hair cut off like a boy?" She said what she felt like saying all the time. Despite how it made the students feel. She was a great teacher and English was my favorite class. I was one of her best students. But, she had a way of putting students in their place whether they deserved it or not. She spoke and asked questions later.

I was totally embarrassed. I mumbled something about getting a natural, that's what my mother called it. But, I didn't tell her any more than that. I couldn't tell her the whole truth. I knew better, my mother forbade telling anything that went on in our house. I don't know how I managed through the rest of that class period. It was the worst day I had had at school ever.

When I left her class I put my hat back on. I was hot. But I kept it on the rest of the day. Somebody on the bus ride home pulled it off my head and threw it out the window. It landed in a muddy ditch.

I was mad but I didn't take up for myself because my mother would get mad if I got in trouble. Her punishment was worse than the event itself and she'd bring it up every time she got upset about something.

The next day my hat was stuck in the mud in the ditch. The bus driver got it out and gave it to me. I never wore it again.

That weekend, my mother took me to the barber shop, I couldn't believe I was going to the same barber shop that she took my brothers to. It was another blow to me. I was called a boy by her and my brother made fun of me too. They laughed together. That was one of her tricks, she'd pit us against each other. Trying to get one to join in with her making fun of the other.

I never would join in with her teasing of my brother no

matter how mad I got with him because I knew how that made me feel and I didn't want any part of it.

She'd called him "peel head, bald head, and black gorilla." "Dumb, stupid, crazy, and lazy." Her favorite name for him was "black gorilla". He didn't appreciate her calling him names but he didn't take it as hard as I did when she talked about me. I was the butt of her boy jokes and her bald head name calling for a long time. She went from that to calling me "crazy", saying I needed help. That was her last resort when she felt I was on to her games.

7 BLOSSOMING

My hair grew back. I eventually got a box permanent that I put on at the kitchen sink with barely enough water to rinse the chemicals out.

I learned how to style my hair with the help of my aunt.

In eighth grade my life started to change, at school anyway. I was still at Walker and enjoying my classes. I had a best friend, we talked and laughed during the school day. Her phone number was long distance so I couldn't talk to her when we weren't at school.

She was very fashionable and smart. I admired her style. She lived only a few miles from the school and we rode the same bus. I learned a lot about style from watching her.

I learned to coordinate my clothes, adding hand me downs to the three outfits that my mother bought me at the beginning of each school year. I had one pair of wedge shoes that I got from Kmart that I wore until the heels were uneven. My aunt gave me stylish earrings and bought me a cute purse.

At school I had friends, I had fun, and I loved learning.

My teachers, including the outspoken English teacher, were supportive and encouraged me to excel. I was becoming more sure of myself even as my mother was tearing me down at home. To look at me, a person might not know that we suffered.

Ninth grade was a complete blossoming. I became popular. I was one of the smart girls and boys my age and older were trying to get my attention. But, I didn't have any feelings for any of them. That changed the next year when I met one young man my age from Magnolia School.

He was tall, bowlegged, that was a big deal for the girls back then, a football player, and he was smart. I thought he was the most handsome boy I had ever seen.

It was the summer before tenth grade that we were told that we would be transferring to Emerson school in the fall because of the district lines or something.

I liked Walker but, I looked forward to the new school, a new experience. I had not gone to school with white students since leaving Chicago when I was in the first grade.

But one thing my mother did do was enjoy white people. She actually had more in common with the white people we saw on television than she did with the black people in our community. She rarely socialized with folks in our community and she used white people on television with their clear pronunciations, ways of dressing, and cultural intelligence as examples of how we should act. She did use Sidney Poitier, Cicely Tyson, and other famous black people as examples too. She looked to people who had accomplished things in their lives as role models for us.

We were only allowed to listen to the local white radio station, easy listening music she called it. We were forbidden to talk slang or watch ethnic shows except for Sanford and Sons occasionally. She hated "Good Times" because of the way they acted. She wouldn't allow us to use incorrect grammar, and even though she had her own brand of madness, she taught us how to act respectably in any situation.

I kept in touch with my classmates from Walker. They were an important part of my life, my growing up. We were considered one of the best classes to go through that school. My teachers were excellent. They prepared me well. I had no problems academically or personally blending in with the students at Emerson. It was one of the best times of my life the three years I was there. I separated my home life from my school life. School was an escape for me. A welcomed relief.

It was at a basketball Jamboree, my first year at Emerson, that I met the person who would be the love of my life even beyond graduation. It took me years to get over him. I had become close friends with a female classmate. We hit it off soon after I arrived at Emerson. Since she lived in the 547 prefix, we could talk in the evenings without it being long distance. We became best friends. The guy I met was her nephew.

He sat next to us at the Jamboree. We talked and had fun the whole game. When it was over, he walked me to my aunt's car. She had come to pick me up. She was living at the house with us while she looked for her own place. He asked me for my phone number. He called me about twice a month. I had to talk very quietly so my mother could not hear me on the phone. I was in love, though I never told him that, we never used those words. We just said we really liked each other. We were never a couple. Later he had a girlfriend even though he was still calling me. I hoped they would break up.

We talked about everything, he was smart and could make me laugh, he could make anything funny. He told me when he would be coming to a basketball game or the Chili Supper in Emerson so we could see each other. It hurt that he didn't choose me to be his girlfriend. I was just a friend to him.

I had a boyfriend in the eleventh grade, he went to

school at Emerson. He was a track star and dressed well. He was kind and wanted to get married someday. He was the only guy who drove to my house to pick me up. He took me to the school dance, our version of a prom. He drove a truck with loud pipes. He had a nice family, I loved his mother. They had cookouts at his aunt's house in Magnolia and always invited me. It was my first time experiencing family events that were not my own family. They treated me like family.

But, I didn't feel the same way about him as he did about me. I liked his devotion and respect. I broke up with him that summer.

In my senior year, I dated who I thought was the most popular guy at Walker. He was in a popular family, and lived near the school. He was tall, well built, sure of himself, and attractive. But, he wouldn't drive to my house. He said it was too far in the woods. We started talking at a basketball game. That was the meeting place back then for students. We watched the game but more importantly, we saw the person we were interested in talking to.

My aunt had moved into a trailer about two miles outside of Magnolia. I could spend the weekend with her. The guy from Walker visited me there or picked me up to go to a game. I was thrilled to be talking to a popular, older guy. He was a year older than me. We were together for several months, we only kissed. Nothing more. He never tried anything. I was still a virgin and wanted to stay that way.

We were in a relationship when I graduated. He came to my graduation, I still have the pictures. I broke up with him a few days later because I did not have strong feelings for him and we didn't have much in common. Even though he said he wanted to continue the relationship, I felt his heart wasn't really in it. We are still friends.

My mother didn't approve of me having friends not to mention a boyfriend. I kept my personal life to myself.

My best friend and I talked about everything. We couldn't wait to get to school to catch up on what we missed, which was not much, because we talked sometimes in the evenings too. We were as close as sisters. I told her everything, except about my home situation. I didn't talk to anyone about that. We just had fun together. We grew apart after I moved away.

I graduated number three in my class of twenty nine. I would be leaving for the Air Force in three months.

8 LEAVING HOME

I sat back in my seat on the jet. I breathed in and exhaled slowly. I was on my way. I didn't know how unprepared I was. Being away from home didn't help the worthlessness I felt. I carried my mother's voice with me. Her insults, her doubts, her suspicions, her fears, her ridicule, were a part of my thinking. I was a mess. But to look at me, you would never know. My appearance was important to me. I was still acting like I was okay. I had to make it. I had nothing to fall back on. I could not depend on anyone else.

I was torn between staying home to help my family, to be a buffer for my little brother and sister and moving away to make a living. It was the hardest choice I had ever had to make. I knew if I stayed at home I would lose my mind and be of no help to myself or them. I had been offered a scholarship to SAU in Magnolia, but I didn't accept it. I wanted to move farther from home and be completely on my own. I was also having trouble concentrating and didn't think I would be able to focus enough to go to college at that time for four years.

We needed money. I needed a full-time job.

If I left and had a paycheck, I could send money home. I could help take some of the burden off my mother financially and maybe she would feel better and do better. But, I was racked with guilt.

I was on a flight to San Antonio, Texas. My first time flying. My first time being that far away from home.

The flight attendant offered me a beverage and small bag of roasted peanuts. I accepted. She poured a sprite in a clear cup and handed it to me. She was pleasant. I was grateful. I had served my mother hand and foot since I was a little girl. I didn't know what it was like to have someone cater to me, even if it was a flight attendant doing her job. It felt really good.

I was on my way to basic training. I had watched films about what to expect. I'd worked out some and was in pretty good shape. I had been through the hardest training already, surviving my mother's abuse. I felt sure I could make it anywhere.

9 AIR FORCE

I was in my third week of basic training when my thoughts started running ahead of me. I felt like I was sprinting to a dead end. Had I made the wrong decision to join the military? It all seemed too hopeless and pointless. I could not see past basic training. The days were long and filled with drudgery and small mindedness of my peers in the barracks. We did everything together, one person could make it hard for my whole squadron. If they fell out of line, we had to make up the slack. Some didn't make it through basic training. We even took showers together. We'd rotate around a large room with shower faucets on the walls, soaping up at one rinsing at another. I hated that. But I did what I had to do.

I liked the marching, the formations, the structure, and the classes. I took pride in folding my t-shirts into six inch squares and shining my shoes as ordered. I kept my area tight.

However, I wasn't used to hearing whining, or pettiness. Sharing a barracks with so many women of all levels of maturity took some getting used. I didn't play around. I was there for one reason, to get through so I could start making a living.

I put my focus on being the best trainee I could be. When I graduated, no family came to my graduation. I never expected anybody too. But I couldn't help but wonder, as I looked at the parents who did come, what it must feel like to have that kind of support.

I packed my things and boarded the chartered bus for technical school. I was glad basic training was over but even as the bus pulled away and I was riding to my future, I was filled with dread. I knew there would be more pretending ahead because I was miserable inside. I second guessed every decision.

Her voice, my mother's voice began to take over. Not harshly or with force but with a quiet authority, "You aren't anything, you aren't ever going to be anything." "You are a fool!" "Look at you, everybody is talking about how stupid you are." "You're crazy!"

The bus ride would be hours. To drown out the thoughts, I put my headphones on and played my Walkman. I had one old cassette tape that I owned. It was so worn out that the words had rubbed off. We had checked our personal belongings in for storage the first day we arrived. They had just given them back to us.

I laid my head back on the seat, listened to the music and tried to imagine how good my life was going to be.

At technical school, the tapes kept running in my mind around the clock. I felt heavy. It was if I was carrying a twenty pound bag of potatoes on my back every day.

My mind was bogging down. I was struggling to keep my sharpness. Easy lessons were requiring more deliberate work. I was sad a lot. I was sleepy all the time even with eight hours sleep. To stay awake, I would take one NoDoz caffeine tablet each morning just before classes began. They worked better for me than the coffee that was available at our breaks. Some classmates had told me about the caffeine tablets that could be bought over the counter. I bought a box at the Base Exchange.

I had a roommate from Syracuse, New York. She had a big smile and we talked for hours sometimes in our barracks. She was attached to me and I enjoyed her company. We shared stories about our siblings, missing them and concerned about them. She had had a rough life too.

Our squadron marched to class in formation each morning, our classroom was on the other side of the base, across flight lines, the wind was whipping, and it was cold.

I was at Sheppard Air Force Base in Wichita Falls, Texas. I was there from around the second week in October through about the second week of December 1986. I graduated with honors.

I trained to be a medical administrative specialist. I had scored highest on the clerical part of my ASVAB test prior to enlisting. I felt comfortable with anything clerical, so administration was a great fit and working in a hospital was a bonus for me.

We had good instructors. I looked forward to putting what I was learning to use at my permanent duty station. Our technical school base was large with state of the art facilities. Everything we needed was there. It was like a city within a city. On the weekends, my roommate and I took the city bus that had a bus stop on the base, to the mall. It was at the salon at the mall where I first got my hair cut like Anita Baker. She had a beautiful and stylish short haircut.

After technical school, I went home on leave for two weeks. I was excited about seeing my little brother and sister. I had talked to them on the phone and exchanged letters. I had made arrangements for my youngest aunt to check on them regularly. I sent her money for their needs. I missed them. I worried about them.

I took them Christmas gifts and Air Force souvenirs. They were always glad to see me, making me feel like I was the greatest person in the world. I was happier to see them.

It was during this leave that I also flew to Kansas City, Missouri to meet my father for the first time. My mother had found him while I was in technical school and arranged for us to meet. I was not excited about this initially.

I resisted because the idea of meeting him at that stage in my life was not necessary for me. I was trying to focus on starting my career without drama. She talked me into it, even trying to make me feel guilty for not wanting to meet my father.

This was the beginning of the tricks she tried to play on me as an adult. She was still manipulative. But, I still cared about her and tried to help her.

Because I wasn't interested in meeting my father, she made a big deal about it. When I had wanted to meet him as a young girl, she demeaned me calling me ignorant. She said I was ungrateful for what she had done for me and that my father had done nothing all my life. Now, when I was on my own and over the whole thing, she insisted I divert my attention to her new endeavor. I agreed to meet him.

My flight landed in Kansas City. I had talked to my father on the phone. He didn't sound the way I'd imagined. He sounded shady to me. I had a description of him but we passed each other at the airport without knowing it. He was a lot shorter and skinnier than I had imaged. He had a Jheri Curl, and a goatee. His teeth looked ragged. He wore a leather jacket, slacks, and dress shoes. He was bright skinned as we call black people who have lighter complexions.

He didn't look like he'd been taking care of himself. He wasn't particularly attractive.

We walked past each other before we realized it. From

first sight, I had a funny feeling about him.

It wasn't long during that visit that he tried to change how I looked. I guess he wasn't impressed with me either.

He took me to the beauty shop that he owned and where my stepmother worked. He had her fix my hair, adding weave to the back to make it look long. He commented about my skin. I was still having breakouts but I was using acne medications to help with it.

He was trying to make me into something else, his idea of what I should be like. He asked what my blood type was and some more questions designed in some way to confirm that I was his daughter. I answered and asked him questions as well, not trying to figure out if he was my father, but what had attracted my mother to him. I could not see it. I felt nothing for him but thought I'd try to get to know him better.

He shared a beautiful home with his wife and my two step sisters, whom I liked

His mother lived several miles away in a small home on a hill, not far from a major freeway. She lived by herself, her husband had passed away years earlier. She wasn't overly friendly, but hospitable. She said she knew about me when I was a little girl, my mother had sent a picture. My father knew about me then too. He never said why he didn't respond to my mother's letter back then. I really didn't appreciate that. I was ready to go. I couldn't wait for my flight back home.

His mother and I talked in her small kitchen at the table and she showed me her photo album. I saw pictures of his father and siblings. She gave me some potholders that she had knitted. I only saw her that one time. We hugged and said goodbye. Her name was Francis.

I met some of his siblings and their children later during that visit. My father took me on a tour, showing me where his siblings lived and introduced me to their families. They were all kind to me. But, I didn't have a feel a connection with my father. He had a way of blaming others for things that were in his control. I kept hoping I'd see something that showed me he had some depth, some quality that I could respect. I thought I'd leave the lines of communication open and maybe come back to visit another time if only to see my new siblings and my stepmother.

I was glad when I returned to Arkansas to finish my leave before heading to my permanent duty station. It was hard to leave my siblings again. I promised to come back every weekend that I could.

Starting my career...

I arrived at England Air Force Base in Alexandria, Louisiana in January of 1987. I moved into the barracks and began work immediately at the base hospital. My first job was as an admin clerk in medical records.

I worked there for about two months. About that time I was recommended for a job with more responsibility in the orderly room. I worked there until I was recommended to do the hospital metrics reporting in medical resource management.

I was replacing a staff sergeant who was going to another base. The reports were a major responsibility, but he had no doubts about my abilities. He trained me step by step on how to compile the information for the reports which were sent to our command headquarters in Langley, Virginia.

He taught me how to do my work without being stressed out about it. He had a great sense of humor, a gentle spirit and loved to listen to old soul music. He was a big influence on me as a supervisor and a friend.

When he left, I was took his place. He had been in charge of our department, reporting directly to our captain. I was the noncommissioned officer in charge of medical resource management. That was a big move for me. I had recently become a sergeant, Sgt. Bennett. I was really proud of that. I had graduated from the noncommissioned officer's leadership school among the top of my class.

I had earned a reputation of being an excellent worker. I learned fast, I was polished, taking extra care in my appearance and uniform, and performed all tasks with the highest degree of professionalism. I studied the manuals and regulations in my spare time to understand all aspects of my job. I received awards and distinctions.

I was also a member of the volunteer Honor Guard. That was a sacred part of my Air Force experience.

In my department, I learned every job. Cross training was part of how we worked. I could do any job in our department, and did them seamlessly during transitions of employees, military and civilian. My main jobs were compiling hospital metrics and doing medical evacuation and temporary duty orders. I was the point of contact for anyone traveling to another base for medical care or temporary duty assignments. I learned a lot about military bases all over the country. I enjoyed talking to the military men and women as they picked up their orders. I knew everybody in the hospital.

I filled in as the discharge clerk and cashier for co-payments for inpatients. All patients came to the cashier's office before leaving the hospital. I was quick and provided great customer service. I filled in for an extended time when our discharge clerk retired. She was a sweet lady who golfed every chance she got and traveled with her husband. I missed her when she retired.

When the sergeant who did CHAMPUS was reassigned and before her replacement arrived, I stepped in to assist with filing CHAMPUS claims, receiving and processing medical bills from hospitals and doctors that active duty members or their spouses used outside of the base for specific reasons.

My office was just across the hall from the squadron commander and the first sergeant. I had worked directly with them when I worked in the orderly room. The hospital commander and the heads of departments were just down the hall. I had great working relationships with them all. They tried to encourage me to make the Air Force a lifelong career. I thought about it.

I could do any job in my field in a moment's notice without missing a beat. That was Air Force training at its best. That was an exciting time for me.

On top of all of that, I was liked and respected by my peers and other superiors. I had great friends, my comrades. We lived in the same barracks on three floors except those who were married who lived in base housing or off base. We ate in the same chow hall that was located a few feet away in the next building. We watched television in the dayrooms that were on each floor of our barracks. Some bought TVs for their rooms, gathering there to watch shows and laugh. We went to the noncommissioned officer's club on Saturday nights, it was just across the parking lot from our barracks, and danced until it closed at 4:00am. We were close. We were like family.

I started taking night classes toward a college degree. One or two classes a semester. We had Saint Leo College and Northwestern State University branches on our base. I had accomplished all this by age nineteen.

But, emotionally, I was struggling with self-doubt. I was distracted at times by negative thoughts caused me to doubt the sincerity of those who cared about me. I was lonely though surrounded by people. I was fearful even though I didn't show it.

I had become disillusioned with church. I had seen so many hypocrites, I had been turned off. I still went to church, off base from time to time, but I didn't have the strong connection and spiritual life I had before leaving home. I didn't smoke or drink and tried hard not to tell a lie or talk about people behind their backs.

My closest friends, the two civilians that I worked with every day, called me "goody two-shoes." But, like everybody else, I had my faults. I would be tested in a way I never imagined.

I felt like I needed someone to love me. I made my first bad relationship choice.

My first marriage ended in divorce. We had had a tumultuous relationship, I had broken up with him at least twice. But each time, he worked his way back into my life.

I was two months from being twenty on the day I said I do in front of a justice of the peace with one witness, my close friend and Air Force buddy from Florida. She lived on the first floor of my barracks and had seen the good and the bad of my relationship with the man I was marrying. She had a soft spot for him, always taking his side when I complained about his behavior. I could see the signs in him, controlling and jealous. I broke up with him and he ripped up all of the things that he had bought me, the stuffed animals, the shirt, and the cards. Anything he saw in my room that night. I called the base police to make him leave. He was told to stay a certain distance from me. He would park across the parking lot and sit in his car with the door open reading a newspaper when he was off duty. After his time was up and he could see me again, he apologized and pleaded with me to give him another chance. I resisted. He pleaded. I eventually agreed to see him again.

I was needy, and he knew it. Despite my outer image, my self-esteem was low. He did everything he could to present himself as a good, loving, supportive man. I knew I was making a mistake when I said I do. It was just the first of a slew of relationship mistakes.

The marriage was my desperate attempt to calm the voices of self-doubt that had tormented me since leaving home. To quiet my mind. He was contrite, promising to never disrespect me again. He was loyal. Steady. Until I married him.

Shortly after we were married, he became possessive. All consuming. Demeaning me if I wanted some space, even a little space to think, to relax, to take a long bath. He wanted to know my every move and waited until I was done so we could resume being together.

If I said that I needed time to be by myself, he was suspicious and accused me of all sorts of things. It was us or nothing. He was in good spirits as long as he could fill our conversations with what was wrong in the world. I felt like I was in a closed box, muffled with cotton. Everything was in slow motion. He was concerned about himself and our life together was centered on him. All my hard work to get where I was meant nothing to him. He was more concerned about his outfits and dancing at the club on weekends. He had no ambitions. He required total attention, constant devotion. I felt like we had been married for years, it was only two months. It was depressing for me.

That Christmas, we had driven to visit his family in another state. He got mad at me over a small thing like he was prone to do, while we were at a party at his cousin's house. It was a small party in a beautiful home with family and friends.

He walked out on me after telling me off, he left me there. I didn't know anyone there. After some time, he came back. He apologized, again like he did after a blow up over nothing. That was our relationship, drama. I said to myself when I get back home to our apartment, I was leaving him.

He was so sweet that I second guessed myself. My folks in Arkansas, the women, were religious and would take extreme amounts of disrespect and stay in a marriage. My complaints about him were dismissed as me being too picky, not being forgiving enough.

I stayed two more weeks. Then one night he was going on and on about some minor thing and I went into the guest room and closed and locked the door. I had to get some sleep for work in the morning. He kicked the door in. He professed his love for me. I left the next day.

10 FAMILY BACK HOME

I moved back into the dorm one day when he was at work. A sergeant who worked in the hospital and knew my situation, helped me. I put my furniture in storage. I filed for divorce. I resumed my friendships that he had come between. I started exercising and eating better, getting proper rest, and enjoying life. I also started back taking night classes toward a degree in business. I planned to go to law school after graduation. I wanted to be a corporate attorney. I was planning to have the life I had dreamed of so many years ago looking up at the tree tops in the back woods of Emerson.

I was glad to be able to focus on myself, my wellbeing, my future.

Around that time, the situation back home in Arkansas was getting worse. My mother was not taking care of my siblings.

I had bought my own car and drove the three hours home at least twice a month. The house was a total disaster, almost unrecognizable from when I lived there.

All the dishes were dirty, trash was everywhere. In the kitchen, food was splashed on the walls and the floor, looking like it hadn't been cleaned in months. The shelves and counter tops were in disarray. The kitchen table was cluttered with all kinds of stuff.

The ceiling in the living room, above the gas heater, was turning dark brown from the fumes. It dipped down in the center as if it would fall in any minute.

The well was too low to have adequate running water. The water that did come through was murky, almost unsuitable for use, definitely unsuitable for drinking. I had set up allotments for two of my aunts, one to pay for the fresh water that I had delivered from a bottled water company to the house.

The other allotment was set up for my aunt who was married, lived in Emerson, and who would take them to see the doctor. It paid for my siblings' medical and dental care. It also paid for my sister's optometry visits and new glasses. She said it was her teacher who noticed she was having trouble seeing at school. I tried to cover everything for them. I also sent my mother money each month and bought supplies when I went home.

I used the majority of my checks to help them because I didn't want them to go through what I did. And even with that, my mother would not provide adequate care for them. She pulled away from them and almost completely stopped taking care of them and the house.

Although there were a lot of canned goods and boxes of dried goods strewn everywhere in the kitchen, they were outdated. They looked like things that had been donated to them. She didn't cook for them. They were left unsupervised some days when she went to work on weekends.

My sister said things were bad when I was not there. She begged me to take her with me as I prepared to go back to my base.

It was heart breaking. I went back to my base wondering how I could help them. I worried more. I could not stop thinking about their situation. I went back the next weekend. I took them with me that time.

I found a one bedroom apartment and we moved in. My sister and I shared the bedroom and my brother slept on the couch in the living room. My other brother had graduated from high school and was attending college and working in central Arkansas. He didn't come home often.

After I took my sister and brother to live with me, my mother was extremely upset and called me all kinds of names. She said I was out of line, that what I was doing was wrong.

I struggled to keep going. I just couldn't stand by and let them be neglected. It was a financial struggle too. I had enough money for us but I had to stick to a tight budget.

I had paid a high price for my mother's anger at herself and the world. She had a habit of taking out her rage on her children. My siblings were beginning to pay too. Without me there, she didn't have a target. She didn't have a servant. She didn't have anyone to pick up the slack and keep the house running smoothly. To keep things from falling apart.

A few months later, I found a house to rent for me and my siblings. It was large, with three bedrooms. They were enrolled in school, both in junior high. I took them to school each morning then went to work at the base hospital. I had gone to the JAG office on base for legal advice. A military attorney explained the steps necessary to file for legal guardianship. He told me to seek a civilian attorney to assist me. I did. She helped me file the paperwork.

I went through the process and after a period of time, I was awarded legal guardianship. My mother was furious. She did not respond to the legal documents, I may have been granted guardianship by default.

My oldest aunt called me to see what was going on. She never called us once to check on us when I was growing up. She never made sure we had food or anything else.

My mother had contacted her crying about me taking away her children. Never a word about what she had done to us. She was the victim.

My aunt talked to me like I was the one in the wrong. I told her what her sister had been doing and she said "I don't believe that." I never felt the same way about her again.

We were all alone, my siblings and I, trying to make a life out of the mess we had lived in for so long. I felt ostracized from the family. My mother had everyone convinced that she was a helpless victim, wanting her children back. My family treated me like I was overreacting. The tradition was to tolerate abuse. Keeping up a front and sweeping stuff under the rug was how problems were dealt with.

I wasn't the only child in my family with low self-esteem. My cousins struggled too. Some became sexually promiscuous, with several unplanned pregnancies in our family. Or they used alcohol or drugs. Some led two lives, quiet and obedient at home and a different person in the streets.

Religion was like a weight, dragging us down with restrictions, don't do this and don't do that, without explanation or healthy alternatives. We were expected to "get saved", especially the girls, to stop wearing pants and don't even start wearing makeup.

We were given religious answers for everything at the expense of common sense or normal physical and emotional development. We had to act like we were not interested in the opposite sex and made to feel guilty, "manish" or "womish" or "fast" as it was called back then. We were expected to go to church all the time. If we didn't, they would say they were "praying for us". If we didn't get saved, "we were going to hell". That was the extent of the life training that most of us received. Even though my mother did not go to church, she prescribed to this mentality. She carried this teaching in her heart and it almost destroyed her. She never forgave herself for having children out of wedlock. She felt shame when she could have felt joy at being a mother. She never allowed herself to live beyond her sanctified teaching even when she was not actively practicing it.

As I listened to my aunt deny my reality, I thought of all of this.

I kept moving forward. It was a very difficult time for me emotionally. But, my siblings were doing well, making friends and getting involved in school activities.

Deployment...

The fall of that year, I received orders to deploy to the Gulf. It was the beginning of the Gulf War.

By then my mother had started seeing a psychiatrist for the first time. She had left the old house and moved about 50 miles away, in with one of her sisters and her children.

Sadly I arranged for my aunt, my mother's youngest sister to take care of my siblings' financial needs again. She had been supportive throughout the whole time, visiting us in Louisiana when she could, and always sending us an encouraging letter or card.

I set up a new allotment in her name for my siblings. She was close to them and knew their needs.

I was somewhat relieved that they could be reunited with our mother since she had admitted she had a problem and was seeking professional help. She was also living with her sister who was a nurse and she had her full support.

I deployed shortly after they were back with her.

I hoped that the change in living conditions, the professional help, and support of her sister, would help her get better.

It did not. I found out after deploying, that she had slipped back into her old ways. She had become a master at deception, even with her siblings. She pretended she was getting better in front of her sister she was living with, all the while talking about her behind her back to my siblings. She had fooled everybody again.

With help, she found a house to rent just up the road from her sister. She started to work again at the local nursing home. But, she continued playing mind games with my siblings. By then they were older, and not buying her act. They resisted. She didn't have the control over them she used to have.

She stopped going to treatment soon after my siblings returned to home. She called the psychiatrist crazy, and that he didn't know any more than she did. She called me a fool for saying she needed help. She ridiculed me for bringing her behavior out into the open, saying I was telling folks her business.

I was tired of pretending. The truth was she was sick and needed help.

I didn't know it then but I was suffering from post-traumatic stress before I went to war. The first war had been in my childhood home. It was a battle for my sanity.

11 SEXUAL ASSUALT

My unit deployed to the Gulf the fall of 1990. I had sent my sister and brother back home, regretfully and with a heavy heart. Now it was time for me to do my duty. I was a good soldier.

I was a self-starter, motivated and excited to serve. When we got our orders to deploy, I didn't hesitate. I was proud. I felt capable. My only concern was for my brother and sister. Would they be okay?

I decided it best not to focus on my fears. I had a job to do.

The flight was over 20 hours long. We had a layover in Turkey. At some point we flew over the Nile River. We were fastened in with seatbelts along the interior walls of a large cargo plane carrying pallets of equipment and ISO shelters. The heavy equipment was secured to the floor in the center of the plane.

I was a member of a hospital squadron. Our job was to assemble a fully operational hospital in desert conditions. We did. Once the hospital was up and running, I worked as an administrative tech. I tracked all of the metrics for the hospital which I reported to our headquarters in the U.S. My secondary job was ambulance driver. We drilled for medical evacuations. Preparing for the worse. We each wore a gas mask strapped to our thigh and an auto-injector, a spring loaded syringe with an antidote, in the side pocket of our BDUs. We were instructed to inject ourselves in the thigh in case of chemical war.

When not working at the hospital, we rotated doing eight hour guard duty shifts, armed with an M-16 and night vision binoculars. When not on guard duty, we trained in breaking down our rifles and reassembling them quickly, how to clean them, and put them back together.

I took pride in my job, just like I did back in the states. I did not joke or play around on my off duty hours. I isolated myself from others, choosing to read books instead. In hindsight, my isolation probably made me more vulnerable, easier to single me out.

I read a lot of self-help books that were among the boxes of books donated to us. They were a part of many books that were in a large box in the recreation room. It was there that I was approached by army soldier, he said he was the driver for a commander or some high ranking official. He outranked me. He was tall, attractive, well spoken, with a sense of humor. He pursued me during our off duty time.

He was not the only one. It was normal for women soldiers to be pursued by our male comrades. Not all men of course did that, but many did. Female soldiers had this to contend with. There were some women who were just as horny as the men. They flirted and propositioned the men too. I made sure to distance myself from women who carried themselves in an inappropriate manner.

I was asked to have sex on many different occasions by enlisted men and even some officers while back home at our base and while deployed in the Gulf. Married men and single men. I did have a brief relationship with one man. When I found out that he was a liar, I stopped seeing him.

While deployed, the offers came. I refused. I remember one officer trying to use reverse psychology on me, telling me that I thought I was too good for him. Trying to make me feel bad enough to be with him. He even told me he had a place we could go that was owned by someone from the region. A house where officers and higher ranking officials went for entertainment. I refused. I didn't even want to come across as flirting.

Somewhere during that time, I lowered my standards.

I allowed myself to have feelings for someone. After some weeks, I accepted the army soldier's offer to go for a ride in his superior's vehicle. We were going to ride and talk and come back. I expected some possible light affection, a kiss at most, because we were attracted to each other. But, we were just getting to know each other. I didn't expect nor want anything more.

He had been on his best behavior, considerate, kind, respectful, each time we talked in the recreation area.

The night of the ride, I signed out as we did when leaving the base to go to designated places. We were allowed to leave the base to go to the shopping area in Saudi Arabia, taking the designated military transportation there and back. It was usually a small bus.

I don't remember the reason I wrote down for our trip that night, but I do remember feeling unsure about it. He promised we'd back shortly. Big mistake.

I went with him.

We drove away from the base. He was describing the places we passed as if he had been there before. He drove farther and farther, I told him we were going out to far. He continued to drive until I had no idea where we were or what turns we had taken. He parked the vehicle.

He talked about his plans for us to be together when we got back to the states. I had thought before that night that we might have a future together. But, I was ready to go back to the base.

He moved closer, started caressing me, then kissing. At first it was welcomed, thinking we would fool around a little then go back to the base. He started becoming aggressive. I told him to stop and take me back to the base. He pleaded for me to let him touch me "on the inside of your thigh". I said No. I pleaded with him to take me back to the base. He wouldn't. He continued to plead to let him do more. I told him that I was uncomfortable and I wanted him to STOP. He persisted.

Afraid that if I did not go along with him, he might kill me and leave me in the dessert, I gave in. I let him touch my thigh. He became more aggressive, and forced himself on me. I begged him to STOP. He continued as if he did not hear me. He had unprotected sex with me against my will. I cried the whole time. He did not stop until he was done.

Then he sat back, like he was astonished at what he had done. I got myself together being careful not to provoke him since no one knew where I was. He could have killed me and left me there in the desert. By the way he was acting, I felt he might. I talked calmly to him, as if everything was okay. I just needed him to come back to himself and take me back to the base. After some time, he drove us back.

I had made the worst mistake of my career. I had left the security of my base with a maniac. All I could think about is getting back to the base alive. I was horrified.

He crawled back into the front seat and drove us back to the base without saying a word. I was angry but stayed calm. I was going to report him as soon as I got to safety.

When I got back to my barracks, I cleaned up. I felt terrible. Then, I started blaming myself. I told my roommate what happened.

I told no one else. I started to feel ashamed. I feared that if I reported him he would tell everybody that I wanted it, that I went along. I had gone for the ride with him. But, I had no intention of having sex. I knew my responsibility to my unit. I was a team player. I had lost my head that night. I had very poor judgement to leave the base with him. How could I explain that to my superiors if there was an investigation? I thought I would be ruined.

Two weeks later I became very ill. I was nauseous and felt faint. My energy was low. I was sick every day but not throwing up, just weak. Never having been pregnant, I thought I had a virus. I went to the hospital, my hospital that I was assigned to, the one that I had helped build, to see a doctor. After a urine test, he informed me that I was pregnant. He told me, I guess confidentially, that I could go to Germany to have an abortion. It was like I was in a fog. I thought, this couldn't be happening.

What was I going to do now? I said I didn't want to have an abortion. Plans were made immediately to send me back to the states.

The officer who had propositioned me before, to go to that house with him, the one I wouldn't go with, said to me as I was preparing to take a military flight back to the states, "I can't believe you were with him and would not be with me." I couldn't believe he was so immature. I walked away without saying anything to him. He didn't deserve a reply. He was like many who were having or wanted to have sex while deployed in the Gulf, with the woman possibly taking all the risks. That seemed to be part of the way it was. The female soldiers, especially the young ones, had to protect themselves.

I arrived back in the states in mid-January 1991. I was embarrassed. I didn't have any idea what I was going to do once I got back to my apartment. I thought of suicide. But the thought of how that would affect my sister and brother, convinced me to not consider it.

After a week of leave, I went back to work doing my normal job at the hospital on base. I met with my commanding officer who had been briefed on my situation. He was concerned about my wellbeing. No actions were taken. He thanked me for my service. I resumed my regular duties. I was extremely sick every day. I could barely hold my head up.

I felt worthless and that I would be the same kind of mother that my mother had been to me. Then my father died suddenly. I had met him for the first time four years earlier. My mother had the Red Cross contact my commanding officer to tell me. I felt nothing. It did not matter to me if I went to the funeral. But I went anyway.

I took a flight to Kansas City, Missouri for his funeral. The house was cold and felt empty. I was so sick that after the funeral, that I sat in the big chair near the corner of the living room, slumped over most of the time. I had no energy. I didn't want to talk to anybody, I didn't want to be there. The sound of people talking as they prepared the food for the visitors made my head hurt. And I was consumed with worry. I was overwhelmed.

After years of drinking, my father had died of cirrhosis of the liver.

I was distressed after the funeral. How could I bring a child into the world when both my mother and father were insane and the man I was pregnant by had raped me? I felt hopeless. I had an abortion when I got back home. I had gone with a friend to the clinic two years before. I knew of several women in the military who had had abortions. I had never considered having one before for myself. I had no reason to. I thought I was smart enough to avoid getting myself into a situation where that would be an option. But, rape does not respect smart or pleading or in some cases when it does not risk a woman's life, fighting back. It is a willful act by a maniac. I was not to blame for his actions.

I called the clinic to make an appointment before I left Missouri.

My plane landed back home in Alexandria, Louisiana. My car was at the airport. The next day, I drove myself to the clinic in Shreveport. I stayed overnight in a hotel the day before the procedure. It was an outpatient procedure that required me to stay in the recovery room for several hours before I was released to go home. I called a cab to take me back to the hotel. I was in pain. I was miserable. The next day, I drove back to my apartment. It was Friday so I had the weekend before having to go back to work on Monday.

I told my family that I had a miscarriage because I didn't want to negatively influence my younger siblings. I thought they were too young to know more at that time. One of my aunts, the nurse asked me definitive questions trying to pin down if I actually had a miscarriage. Rumors spread in my family that I had had an abortion. I didn't care. I had to live my own life. When I needed the oldest aunts, when I was growing up, they were not there for me. So why should I be concerned about their judging me now. I had to deal with my choices myself. I had to take care of me.

The next day, the guilt was overwhelming. I started seeing a therapist. I was twenty two.

12 PICKING UP THE PIECES

With help from the therapist, I forgave myself. I learned coping skills that at least on the surface were enough to keep me living. I was still working on building my self-esteem. I focused on my work.

I still had a heaviness and guilt that I carried with me. I started back taking night classes toward my degree. But, I was having trouble concentrating. I was failing Algebra. I went into a self-blaming mode that prevented me from seeing that it was a temporary setback and that I could study harder and get different results. I was very hard on myself.

All I could hear in my mind was, "You are a failure!" "You are a worthless failure!" The tapes kept running over and over in my head.

I went home that weekend to check on my siblings. I met my daughter's father there. My aunt who was married to his uncle invited us both to her house for dinner the night after I arrived. He had seen a picture of me on my aunt's end table in her living room. He said he thought I was beautiful. He wanted to meet me.

He talked intelligently, but laughed at his own jokes. He was skinny, dressed in a white cotton t-shirt and old jeans. He was on leave from the Navy, in between duty stations on his way to teach at Great Lakes Naval Base in North Chicago. He was a corpsman and had worked seeing patients in the clinic at his base and while out to sea.

He said that his last duty station was in San Diego. He said he had lived off base there in a nice home with his wife and two sons, before they divorced.

He was about five feet eleven with dark black coarse hair that he wore low, brushed, with small waves. He was somewhat attractive with a gorgeous smile. He was easy to talk to and hardly took his eyes off me the whole evening. My aunt fixed pork chops, biscuits, and gravy. We ate and laughed. We had a good time.

At the end of the evening, as I was preparing to go to my mother's house, he asked if he could call me when he reached his new duty station. I said yes. I thought it would be nice to get to know him. After all he was divorced. So I thought.

He was my aunt's husband's nephew. She had invited us both to dinner. I believed that if he was a bad guy, they would have told me. If he was still married, my aunt would have told me. Instead, they laughed and joked along with him while we had dinner at their house.

He said he was applying to medical school in the near future. I wondered how or why he would do that at his age, he was thirty three. That didn't make sense to me. But, it was better than some of the conversations I've heard people trying to impress me talk about.

I knew he was in the Navy, and a corpsman. That he said he loved his sons and planned to share in raising them with his ex-wife. That his sons would live with him in base housing and go to their home in Muskegon, Michigan with his ex-wife two weekends out of a month. He visited his elderly parents often in Muskegon and had high regard for them. My aunt knew him. That was enough for me. I had my own career plans and he was interested in them, encouraging me to go for the highest.

Once he arrived at his new base, he called me. After talking to each other every night after my classes for weeks, we began a long distance romance.

We talked of marriage, what he was looking for in a wife, what I was looking for in a husband.

It wasn't long before we thought we were in love. He asked me to spend the rest of my life with him. He wanted me to move in with him when I got out of the military.

Determined that I would not become pregnant without being married, I told him we would have to be married for me to move in with him. I set a date. He agreed. Things moved fast.

I took flights to see him in Chicago and he flew to see me in Louisiana. He wrote me long love letters. I did not write him letters. His letters were detailed, caring, and loving. He said he loved me and that we were a perfect fit for each other. That I was everything he wanted and he was blessed to have me in his life. I felt I loved him, but I was not as emphatic as he was. We made plans to be married that September. The wedding would be small.

In April of that year, our base was notified that it would be closing at the end of that year. It was a part of the reduction of U.S. armed services that was taking place in 1992.

I was given the option of taking an assignment to Greensboro, North Carolina or taking an early out.

I took the early out because I wanted to pursue my education full-time.

I received an honorable discharge and became a civilian. I still had plans of becoming a lawyer. I would start college full-time when I was settled in Waukegan, in base housing. He had already moved his young sons there. I was excited about helping him raise the boys.

I worked until June as we sorted and boxed up the medical records for all the personnel on the base in order that they be shipped to other bases or to headquarters for archival.

I processed out, completing all of my required discharge paperwork and relocation forms. I went through the transitional assistance program, preparing for civilian life.

My personal items were packed and moved for me by a moving company hired by the Air Force. They did this for all personnel who were leaving the service unless they chose to do it themselves and be reimbursed. They moved my things to my brother's house in Pine Bluff, Arkansas. For some reason I sent my things there, maybe intuition.

My fiancé took a flight down to help me drive to our home in Illinois.
Not long after I arrived, he bought me a princess cut diamond engagement ring. The very one I wanted. However, as the time approached for us to discuss the wedding plans, he made excuses to postpone the date. I realized I had moved too soon. That because I was still looking for validation from someone other than myself, I was in another bad relationship.

Shortly after that, he confessed that he was not divorced. He was separated from his wife and in a nasty custody battle over his sons. They were also in a battle over the proceeds from the sale of the home they owned together. It was constant drama between him and his wife as they fought through the divorce. I hated it. I needed peace.

He wanted things to stay the same between us. To just live together. I didn't want that. Our relationship turned negative. We argued a lot. I was upset and felt betrayed. He had no regrets and wanted to keep things the way they were. We became distant. I finally woke up. I stopped looking for him or anybody else to do for me what I could do.

I decided to leave and go back to Arkansas. I had planned to be in my hometown area for a short time then get a job in administration in another state and relocate there. Three weeks later I found out that I was pregnant. I was physically sick again and I was jobless and didn't have a place of my own. But, that time, I was determined to have my child no matter what it took.

When I left him, I was not aware that I was pregnant. I was surprised because I had had a light menstrual cycle during that time. But, I was happy. I felt that the baby and I would be okay. Even though my savings was running out and I had not found a job or gotten my own apartment. I had faith that everything we needed would be provided. I would get a job, I would take care of us.

I called him and told him I was pregnant. He asked, "What do you want me to do about it".

Then he said that I had been seeing someone else and had gotten pregnant by him. That hurt me in a way I had not felt before because I had only been with him.

I told him because he needed to know that he was going to be a father. To give him an opportunity to be in her life. He, unfortunately, was not ready to assume his responsibility.

I had made so many poor choices. But, my baby was not one of them, she was a light in a dark time for me.

I made an appointment with a local doctor to begin my prenatal visits. My aunt and uncle in Emerson let me stay with them. They had a large house and they gave me one of their daughters' rooms. I was grateful but also felt ashamed that I had come back home broke, single, homeless, and pregnant. I felt defeated.

I had not learned how to love myself. I was looking for love in other people. I knew that if I was going to be a success in life, I had to value myself. I could not give my power away. I made up my mind that I would reach my goals for me and my baby.

I pressed forward, getting a part-time job doing income taxes at H&R Block in Magnolia. After my fourth month of pregnancy, the sickness subsided. I felt good physically and emotionally.

I held onto my unborn child, metaphorically, and protected her. I rubbed my belly and talked to her, I promised I would do right by her.

I believed that things would get better. This was the first time I said to myself I was cutting off my mother, completely. I was ending her influence over my life. I couldn't allow her negative words and behavior to affect me. I could not afford to be depressed. Soon I would have a child to raise, I didn't have time for her BS. I drew the line.

I stopped talking to her. I shut her out of my thoughts. I focused on me and my baby.

I would not let anybody keep me from being a good mother to my daughter, not even my own mother.

I put distance between us. I went about my business doing what I had to do.

She fought back with denial and with demeaning remarks to my siblings about me, still trying to divide us. It was too exhausting to even think of her, I made peace within myself that she would not be a part of my life.

My siblings continued to grow and develop individual, creative, and strong, personalities and pursued their own interests. We remained close. My mother ended up living alone with strained relationships with all of us. We love her and respect her, but we also respect ourselves, we keep healthy boundaries.

13 FULL CIRCLE

When I moved back to Arkansas, I had only planned to stay for a few weeks, just enough time to regroup and get a job in another state. I had some great memories of the outdoors of my home state and there were some good people who had helped me along the way. But there were too many bad memories for me. I needed to create my own life in a new place with greater opportunities.

But, it did not turn out that way. I had to adjust my plans. I looked at where I was, what resources I had: my intelligence, my health, my baby on the way, my car, my ambition, my determination, and my work ethic, and my GI Bill.

I would be lying if I said that we lived happily ever after. That is not realistic. It was a challenge. Facing each day with self-confidence, faith, and courage. I was the victor. I lived that way. My muscles were toned by my struggles and made me a more powerful woman.

For the first four years after I had my daughter, it was fast pace with me working, going to college, and taking care of her. I kept my distance from my mother with minimal contact. I went to family gatherings so that my daughter would know her folks. I never liked the gatherings. But she loved her little cousins.

Most of the time my mother didn't attend but the memories of my growing-up was in everything from the pots of greens to the banana pudding. I wanted to forget completely. I learned to disconnect the negative memories from the good ones. That allowed me to be involved in family events occasionally. It allowed my daughter to grow up knowing her relatives. Although I kept a close eye on her even there.

I created our own traditions for birthdays and holidays. I was not dependent on extended family to make me feel connected to my roots. I knew my roots. I was making new ones, as a fully actualized adult. I could love them and still honor my individuality.

Pulling away from my mother was extremely difficult. I had a counselor who helped me sort things out. My brother and sister were older then. Both had graduated from high school and were creating lives for themselves.

The day my daughter was born, I was filled with love and fear. As I laid in my hospital room alone, after I had held her for the first time. Tears flowed down my face.

The fear came flooding in, I thought, "How was I going to raise her in this horrible world?" A world in which I had to protect myself even from my mother. I said a prayer, "Please God, help me raise my child".

Two months later I started college full time and hired one of my aunts to keep Morgan. She was not working and needed the income. She came to my apartment each morning so I did not have to take the baby out.

I dressed her, fed her, and hugged her each morning before I left for class. I told her I loved her. Then I drove to the campus to begin my day. I had scheduled my classes to start early in order to be able to work in the afternoons.

I received the GI Bill to pay my tuition and worked on campus to pay rent. It was me and her. She was a happy baby. I made sure she had the best that I could afford. She did not lack for anything. I had a one bedroom apartment in Magnolia, only minutes from the college. Her baby bed was directly across from the foot of my bed. As she grew and began to pull herself up, she would often be standing, waiting to see me move, then start jumping in the excitement. She was my greatest encourager. My inspiration.

We made it. I graduated two years later with a bachelor's degree in psychology then went on to graduate school.

A year and a half later, I had earned a master's degree in mental health counseling.

My daughter and I celebrated. Shortly after that, I started my first full-time job as a professional, since the military. I was proud to be working for my college alma mater

Morgan was an energetic, fun loving, and smart little girl, pretty with long ponytails and a perfect smile. She gave big hugs and laughed a lot. She was a social butterfly. She liked swimming and girl scouts. She had lots of friends.

She loved playing outside, climbing trees just as I had. There were two trees in the courtyard in front of our two bedroom apartment. We had moved to have more room. She had her own bedroom that I furnished in white wicker, and bought her a small television to play her Disney movies. She would sing along to them all, knowing every word. We sang together.

I had started reading to her when she was born and bought her books often. She loved reading. Pocahontas was one of her favorites. She went to preschool, her teachers were fantastic. She started first grade and we were blessed to have another great teacher, Mrs. Weaver. I was teaching as an adjunct instructor at the college as well as working full-time as a program coordinator. After work, I picked her up from the Montessori after school center, she talked excitedly all the way home. I looked forward to our ride home. I fixed dinner as she played. If I had to prepare for the class I was teaching, she grabbed her book and sat on the couch beside me. We were a great team.

I gave her love, protection, and respect. Everything I didn't have as a child, she had that and more.

EPILOGUE

At the beginning of this book, I asked myself, "How did I get here?" I was distressed and running out of money. I was starting over after a slew of poor choices. Looking back over my life, I answered that question.

I had gotten there by being taught that I was nothing as a little girl and throughout my life at home. That my opinion of myself was secondary to what others thought of me. That I did not belong to myself but was subject to the control of others.

I saw the trajectory of my life as I wrote this book. The missed lessons, the tearing down of my self-esteem. The destruction of hope and the installation of fears. I was a product of my upbringing, wounded before I even started to live my life. But, I am not my past.

Had I known when I was just starting out as an adult how powerful I was, how talented I was, I would have made different choices. I did not know I was worthy. Worthy of love, of respect, or protection. Worthy simply because I existed. That what I made of myself was up to me.

I didn't trust the world as a safe place, I believed there was no place for me. That was an erroneous belief. One that created pitfalls and hopeless thinking that interfered with my ability to make the best choices. That negative belief almost destroyed me. It was a lie.

I asked God to forgive me and I have forgiven myself. That's a wonderful thing.

I have forgiven my mother and now that I have lived my life, I see how brokenness can be inherited, passed down from generation to generation. I had a lot of the behaviors and thinking patterns from my mother, undoubtedly, she inherited some of these behaviors from her father or other family members. Somewhere she had burdened herself with impossible standards that she beat herself up about daily. She devalued her abilities, finding fault in everything she did. She felt helpless to change her situation.

Learned helplessness, a theory I learned in my studies in psychology in college, describes what I believe happened in my family. My mother felt hopeless, she believed that she was unable to change her situation. She became stuck. She became bitter. She passed that way of thinking on to me and no matter how I wanted it to be otherwise, it was a part of me. I had to learn to think and act differently.

I did. I learned to honor myself, my ideas, my abilities and expect good things. I was able to see the world with its ups and downs not as a victim with no control, but as an active agent, moving confidently toward my goals. I had the power through work and faith to direct my life.

I was not alone, the whole time God was with me, is with me. That's how I did not lose hope. He was there even when I thought it was too dark to see. He was guiding me.

Just as helplessness can be learned, it can be unlearned. Remember that.

No matter what you have been taught about yourself, it can be re-taught. With the proper help and support, a professional or a trusted adult with knowledge of your situation and the wisdom to find solutions. Not everybody is qualified to know your past, you manage the revealing of yourself, in time, as you heal. Heal yourself first, then testify, share, if you feel led to do so. But your healing comes first. That's your priority.

Remember, you are in control of you. I am a witness, you can survive and thrive.

Abuse is a sad reality but it can be changed. It can be prevented. Awareness is the first step. Acknowledging this secret cancer in families and creating solutions is imperative. This book is my attempt to shine the light on child abuse and the long term effects. Not all victims have visible scars.

It may take years to overcome abuse. The key is prevention. Supporting healthy families. If it has already occurred, we must surround the children with unconditional love and practical support, not empty words and prayers without action. They need education that is family focused.

We need to redefine community to provide creative spaces and outlets, adequately supervised youth centers even in rural areas, gardens or farms where children and families can produce something while enjoying the outdoors. We need to have places or centers for adults to express their concerns and develop relationships and explore their gifts and talents. A place to relax and recharge. All these things help an otherwise overwhelmed parent to see that they have support and options.

These are some of my ideas, from a child who grew up in an abusive home. I hope to be able to make these ideas into a reality. Some communities already do them. I want to be a part of continuing the work on behalf of healthy families.

I hope that more of us will support healthy families, provide real life, hands on support to those who are hurting, check on our neighbors, put arms around needy children, and all children, give hope to stressed parents.

*Update: All of my mother's children worked our way through college, three served in the military, and two earned master's degrees. All are happy and productive. We all volunteer in our communities. To God be the Glory.

Warmest Regards,
Stephanie

STEPHANIE THOMPSON

ABOUT THE AUTHOR

I was born and raised in Emerson, Arkansas, a small rural town not far from Louisiana. Most of my growing up, we were on welfare. I am the oldest of four children born to a single mother. Our fathers were absent.

I served in the Air Force, earned a master's degree in counseling, worked as a program director, mental health therapist, and I volunteer in my community. I enjoy creating and coordinating programs to help youth reach their potential. I also enjoy cooking and reading.

I am the author of 2 other books: *Down South: A Collection of Recipes*; filled with simple delicious recipes that I learned to make while in the kitchen with my mother; and *Unlikely Billionaire*; a fictional story of a woman's rise from poverty to become a billionaire in the food industry. Both books are available at Amazon.com.

I currently live in Camden, Arkansas with my husband and two children.